The Redhouse Guide

to

THE BLACK SEA COAST

of

TURKEY

by

JOHN FREELY

Photographs by
Anthony E. Baker

Published by the Redhouse Press,
Rızapaşa Yokuşu No. 50, Mercan, Istanbul

© 1996 Redhouse Press
Cover design: Cerina Logico Blakney

ISBN 975-413-070-1

Printed in Turkey by Uycan Yayınları Anonim Şirketi,
Büyükdere Caddesi No. 53, Maslak, Istanbul

FOR BRENDAN

CONTENTS

LIST OF ILLUSTRATIONS

LIST OF ILLUSTRATIONS

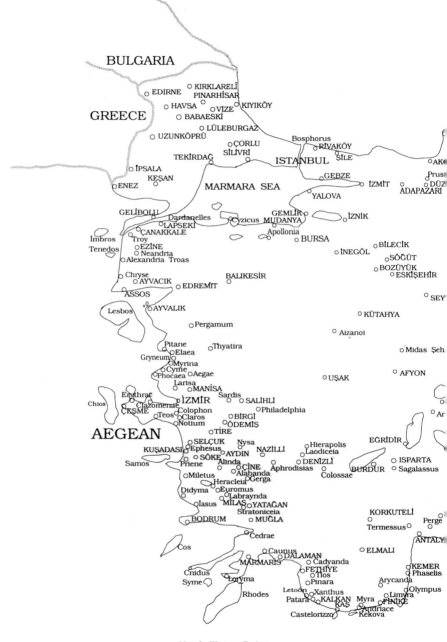

Map I Western Turkey

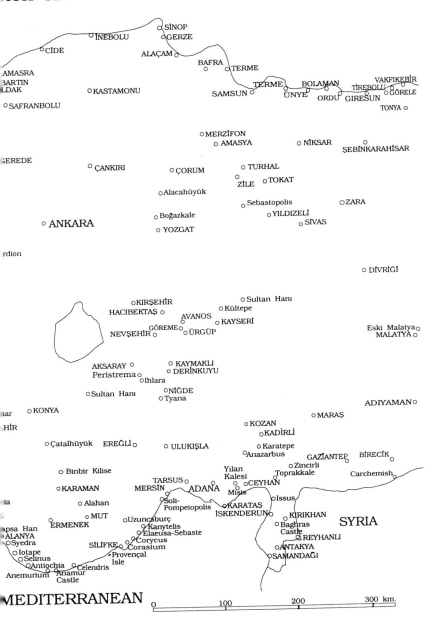

BLACK SEA

MEDITERRANEAN

0   100   200   300 km.

AUTHOR'S NOTE

This is one of a series of guides to the various regions of Turkey. It covers that part of Turkey's Black Sea coast that lies in Anatolia, the Asian part of Turkey. The Black Sea coast of Thrace, the European part of Turkey, will be covered in a subsequent volume of this series. The itineraries detailed in this guide are designed so that the stopping-places are in towns with hotels, which are few and far between along some stretches of the Black Sea coast, a region that is for the most part still undeveloped for tourism. But for the independent traveler this inconvenience only adds to the interest of the journey, giving it the quality of an exploration, one that encompasses some of the most fascinating regions of Turkey.

TURKISH SPELLING AND PRONUNCIATION

Throughout this guide, except in quotes from earlier travelers, modern Turkish spelling has been used for Turkish proper names and for things that are specifically Turkish.

Vowels in Turkish are pronounced as in French or German; i. e., **a** as in f*a*ther, **e** as in m*e*t, **i** as in mach*i*ne, **o** as in *oh*, and **u** as in m*u*te. In addition, there are three other vowels that do not occur in English: **ı** (undotted), pronounced as the "u" in b*u*t, **ö** as in German or as the "oy" in ann*oy*, and **ü** as in German or as "ui" in s*ui*t.

Consonants are pronounced as in English, except for the following:

c as "j" in *j*am, e.g. **cami** (mosque) = jahmy
ç as "ch" in *ch*at, e.g. **çorba** (soup) = chorba
g as in *g*et, never as in *g*em
ğ is almost silent and tends to lengthen the preceding vowel
ş as in *s*ugar, e.g. **çeşme** (fountain) = cheshme

GLOSSARY

The following list includes both the Turkish words and the technical, architectural, and archaeological terms used in the text. The Turkish words in parentheses are the forms which the immediately preceding words assume when modified by a noun, e.g. Yeni Cami (the New Mosque), but Sultan Ahmet Camii (the Mosque of Sultan Ahmet).

abacus the uppermost member or division of a capital

acropolis upper city, usually fortified

ada (adası) island

astragal a small convex molding of round surface

basilica originally a Roman exchange and court of law; in Christian times a church with a central nave and side aisles of lower height

bedesten a Turkish market building usually used for the storage and sale of the most precious goods

beylik a Türkmen principality

burun (burnu) nose, also cape or headland

büyük big

cadde (caddesi) avenue

cami (camii) mosque

capital the topmost member of a column

caravansarai an inn for travelers, caravansary

çay (çayı) tea, also a small stream

çeşme (çeşmesi) fountain

darüşşafaka orphanage

darüşşifa hospital

dağ (dağı) mountain

deniz sea

dere (deresi) stream or valley

dershane lecture hall of an Islamic school of theology

entablature the superstructure carried by a colonnade

GLOSSARY

eski old

ev (evi) house

exedra a semicircular niche

eyvan vaulted room with one side open to a court, iwan

fillet a flat molding separating other moldings; also the space between two flutings in a shaft

frieze the middle element of an entablature; also any horizontal zone adorned with reliefs

Gazi warrior for the Islamic faith

göl (gölü) lake

hamam (hamamı) Turkish bath

han (hanı) Turkish commercial building, sometimes a caravansary

hisar (hisarı) fortress

horon a folk dance of the eastern Black Sea coastal region

imaret Ottoman public kitchen

impost the top member of a pillar

ırmak (ırmağı) river

kale (kalesi) castle or fortress

kapı (kapısı) gate or door

kemençe small violin played like a cello, kemancha

kilise (kilisesi) church

konak (konağı) large house

köprü (köprüsü) bridge

köy (köyü) village

küçük little

külliye (külliyesi) religious complex, usually including a mosque and all of the pious foundations attached to it

kümbet Selçuk mausoleum

kütüphane library

medrese (medresesi) Islamic school of theology, medresseh, madrasah

mescit (mescidi) small mosque, masjid

meydan (meydanı) village square or town center, maidan, meidan

mihrab niche in a mosque indicating the direction of Mecca

mimber the pulpit in a mosque, minbar

mullion a slender bar or pier between lights of a window or screen

GLOSSARY

narthex vestibule of a church

nehir (nehri) river

ogive arch pointed arch

pendentive one of the triangular, curved, overhanging surfaces that make the transition from the circular cornice of a dome to its supporting arches

portico a colonnaded space with a roof supported on at least one side by columns

presbytery that part of a church reserved for the officiating priests

rakı raki, arrack

şadırvan mosque fountain used for ritual ablutions

saray (sarayı) palace, seraglio, serail

şehir (şehri) town

Şehzade Prince

sokak (sokağı) street

squinch a small arch or bracket built across each angle of a polygonal structure to support it over a square or octagonal base

su (suyu) water or stream

synthronon seats for the clergy around the periphery of an apse

tekke (tekkesi) a dervish lodge or monastery

tımarhane insane asylum

triptych a picture or carving in three compartments side by side

türbe (türbesi) mausoleum, turbeh, turbe

tympanum the space enclosed by an arch

yayla summer pasturage and encampment

yeni new

Yürük Turkish nomadic tribespeople

Entrance to the Bosphorus from the Black Sea

Building the Argo, relief in Villa Abani, Rome

CHAPTER ONE

FROM THE BOSPHORUS EASTWARD ALONG THE BLACK SEA

Turkey is bounded on its north by the Black Sea, known in Turkish as Karadeniz, the literal meaning of which is "black sea." The ancient Greeks called it the Pontus Euxinos, or more simply the Euxine, meaning the "hospitable sea," which they did to placate it, for they were terrified by its storms. It was originally known as the Axeinos, a non-Hellenic name which may signify "dark" or "north."

The Asian and European parts of Turkey's Black Sea coast are divided by the Bosphorus, with ninety-three percent of the country's land mass being in Asia and the rest in Europe. The Bosphorus connects the Black Sea with the Sea of Marmara, the Propontis of antiquity, which in turn is linked with the Aegean by the Dardanelles, the Greek Hellespont.

The Asian part of Turkey comprises Anatolia, which in times past was known in the West as Asia Minor. Anatolia is the Greek word for "east," more literally the "land of sunrise." The name *Asia* may have had this meaning in both the Indo-European and Semitic families of languages, while *Europe* may have meant "sunset" or the "land of darkness." The distinction between these two names would have been dramatically evident to ancient navigators making their way up the Bosphorus from the Propontis to the Euxine, with Asia to the east and Europe to the west, the sun rising over the right side of the strait and setting below the left, the deep blue waters of the channel clearly dividing the "land of sunrise" from the "land of darkness."

The first Greek mariners may have ventured into the Euxine late in the Bronze Age, in the thirteenth century B.C., their exploratory voyages perpetuated in the myth of Jason and the Argonauts. The myth begins with the story of Phrixus and his sister Helle, children of Nephele, goddess of the clouds. Their father, King Athamas of Boeotia, was about to sacrifice Phrixus and Helle to propitiate the gods during a time of drought, having been persuaded to do so by the children's evil stepmother, Ino. When Nephele learned of this she flew down from the clouds to save her children, sending them off on a golden-fleeced ram given to her by Hermes. The ram carried them eastward through the heavens, but as they soared over the Dardanelles Helle fell off and was drowned. Thereafter in her memory the strait came to be known as the Hellespont, and to her also the Greek people owe their name of the Hellenes. Phrixus managed to hang on as the ram carried him to the land of Colchis at the eastern end of the Euxine, where he was received with honor by King Aeëtes and wedded to the the king's daughter, Chalciope. As a token of gratitude for his deliverance Phrixus sacrificed the ram to Zeus and gave the golden fleece to Areëtes, who hung it in a grove of trees sacred to Ares, the god of war. The golden fleece was later retrieved by Jason, son of King Cretheus of Pelion and nephew of King Athamas. When Jason set off on his expedition he built a ship called the *Argo,* which was endowed by Athena with the power of speech; and heroes from all over the Hellenic world, including Heracles and Orpheus, volunteered to fill the fifty seats of her rowing benches. They came to be known as the Argonauts, the crew of the vessel that Spenser, in *The Faerie Queene,* called "the wondred *Argo,* which...first through the Euxine sea bore all the flower of Greece." When the Argonauts reached the land of Colchis they were aided by Aeëtes' daughter Medea, who fell in love with Jason and accompanied him on his homeward voyage with the golden fleece aboard the *Argo.* The only full account of the voyage of the *Argo* that has survived is the *Argonautica* of Apollonius Rhodius, written in the mid-third century B.C. But Jason and the Argonauts are mentioned by sources as ancient as Homer, who in *The Odyssey* has Odysseus speak of *"...Argo,* who is in all men's minds."* Pindar refers to the Argonauts in one of his Pythian odes, where he writes of how "Hera kindled sweet desire in the sons of God for the ship *Argo,* so that none should be left behind to nurse a life without danger at his mother's side, but rather that he should find even against death the finest antidote in his own courage along with the others of his age."

The description that Apollonius gives of the Euxine coast is based on that of Xenophon in his *Anabasis,* or *The March Up Country,* written early in the fourth century B.C. The most complete description of the Euxine coast of Anatolia in antiquity is that of Strabo (64 B.C. - ca. A.D. 25), in Books XI and XII of his *Geography.* Strabo would have known the coast well for he was born in Amasia, the ancient capital of the Pontus, a kingdom that comprised the eastern Anatolian coast of the Euxine and its hinterland before Asia Minor came under Roman rule. He also describes Paphlagonia and Bithynia, the two kingdoms to the west of the Pontus, the former occupying the central area of the Euxine coast of Anatolia and the latter the westernmost region, bounded to the west by the Bosphorus and the Propontis.

The Greeks began establishing colonies along the shores of the Euxine in the mid-eighth century B.C., a number of them continuing in existence today as towns and cities in Turkey and other countries around the coast of the Black Sea. They continued founding colonies in the following century in the Euxine, as well as in the straits linking it to the Aegean, one of them being Byzantium, founded ca. 660 B.C. on the European shore where the Bosphorus flows into the Marmara. Constantine the Great made Byzantium the capital of the Roman Empire in A.D. 330, after which it was called Constantinople. This began the Byzantine period of history, which ended in 1453 when Sultan Mehmet II conquered Constantinople and made it the capital of the Ottoman Empire, renaming the city Istanbul. Istanbul was replaced by Ankara in 1923 as the capital of the Turkish Republic, which arose out of the ashes of the Ottoman Empire.

The literature on the Black Sea coast of Turkey is very sparse, both in antiquity and in modern times. And the few sources are all concerned with the Black Sea coast of Anatolia, while virtually nothing is written about the coast of Turkey in Europe, west of the

4 *FROM THE BOSPHORUS EASTWARD*

Bosphorus. The earliest description of the Bosphorus is by the French scholar Petrus Gyllius, whose work was published posthumously in 1561. Gyllius identified a number of places on the Bosphorus associated with the myth of Jason and the Argonauts, and some of these can still be seen today. The most detailed description of the Black Sea coast of Anatolia in the later Ottoman period is that of William J. Hamilton, in his *Researches in Asia Minor, Pontus and Armenia* (2 volumes, London, 1842). The most important modern work on the region is that of Anthony Bryer and David Winfield, *The Byzantine Monuments and Topography of the Pontus* (2 volumes, Wahington, D.C.,1985). All of these works will be referred to and quoted in the chapters that follow.

The sites that Gyllius identified with the mythical voyage of Jason and the Argonauts are all on the upper Bosphorus. One of these is the ruined fortress known as Yoros Kalesi on the Asian shore above Anadolukavağı, the last ferry stop on that side of the strait. This is opposite Rumelikavağı, the last ferry stop on the European side. The shore highway ends at these two points, but on each side of the strait another road leads inland along the ridges above to the villages at the mouth of the Bosphorus.

Yoros Kalesi is a Byzantine fortress known in English as the Genoese Castle. This name comes from the fact that from the late thirteenth century until the Turkish conquest of 1453 it was in the hands of the Genoese. The highest point of the fortress is the hill known as Yoros Tepesi, which commands a dramatic view of the entrance to the Bosphorus from the Black Sea, eight kilometers to the north as the eagle flies. According to Gyllius, Yoros Tepesi was the site of the temple of Zeus Ourious, god of the favoring wind, where there was also a hieron, or sacred precinct, dedicated to the twelve Olympian gods. Gyllius was led to his identification by the name Yoros, doubtless a corruption of Ourious. According to one version of the myth, the temple was founded by Phrixus, who stopped here to offer sacrifice to Zeus after his sister Helle lost her life in falling from the flying ram into the Hellespont. Another version has it that the sanctuary was founded by Jason, who stopped here on his way home from Colchis with the golden fleece. Whoever its founder was, this was undoubtedly the temple that Herodotus mentions in connection with the bridge of boats that Darius built across the Bosphorus in 512 B.C., at the outset of his campaign against the Scythians. While the bridge was under construction Darius sailed up the Bosphorus to visit the sanctuary here and see the entrance to the strait, as Herodotus writes in Book IV of his *History:* "Here, seated in the temple which stands by the straits, he looked out over the Euxine, a sight indeed worth seeing."

There is an even better view of the entrance to the strait from Yuşa Tepesi, the Hill of Joshua, the wooded peak just to the south of Anadolukavağı. The peak was known in antiquity as the Bed of Hercules, but from late Ottoman times onward Western travelers have called it the Giant's Grave. The giant in question is a Muslim saint called Yuşa, whom some pious Turks believe to be the Prophet Joshua; his supposed grave is some twelve meters long and marked by green-painted stellae at his head and feet. The saint's grave has now become a very popular place of pilgrimage, with a mosque erected beside the walled enclosure in which he is buried. The view from the summit is superb, with all of the upper Bosphorus in sight. Lord Byron came here for the view during his visit to Istanbul in the spring of 1810 and described what he saw in a memorable canto in *Don Juan:*

> The wind swept down the Euxine, and the wave,
> Broke foaming o'er the blue Symplegades,
> 'Tis a grand sight from off the Giant's Grave
> To watch the progress of these rolling seas
> Between the Bosphorus, as they lash and lave
> Europe and Asia, you being quite at ease:
> There's not a sea the passenger e'er pukes in,
> Turns up more dangerous breakers than the Euxine.

The Symplegades that Byron refers to are the famous Clashing Rocks, also known as the Cyanean Rocks because of their blue-green color. These were the dreaded obstacles that wrecked ships at the mouth of the strait, and the Argonauts were warned of them when they visited King Phineus in his palace on the upper Bosphorus. Gyllius identified the site of his palace as Garibiye Burnu, a promontory on the European shore three kilometers from the Black Sea. There is a fairly well-preserved Ottoman fortress on the headland above the cape; this was built in 1773 for Sultan Mustafa III by Baron de Tott, a French military engineer in the Turkish service.

The ancient name of this place, according to Gyllius, was Gyropolis, the Place of Vultures. It received its name from the myth of King Phineus, the blind old prophet who was the son-in-law of Boreas, god of the north wind. It seems that Phineus was tormented by the harpies, winged female monsters who, every time a meal was set before the king, would swoop down upon the food and snatch most of it away, leaving the remainder possessed of such a loathsome stench that it was inedible. As a result, Phineus had almost wasted away by the time that Jason and the Argonauts

Anadolukavağı and the Genoese Castle

arrived on their journey up the Bosphorus. Among them were Zetes and Calais, the winged sons of Boreas, who took pity on Phineus, their brother-in-law. When the harpies descended to torment Phineus they were driven away by Zetes and Calais and never returned. The grateful Phineus responded by advising the Argonauts about the rest of their journey, particularly about how to make their way past the fearsome Cyanean Rocks at the entrance to the Bosphorus. As Apollonius quotes Phineus in *The Argonautica:*

When you leave me, the first thing you will see will be the two Cyanean Rocks, at the end of the strait. To the best of my knowledge, no one has ever made his way between them, for not being fixed to the bottom of the sea they frequently collide, flinging up the water in a seething mass which falls on the rocky flanks of the straits with a resounding roar. Now as I take it you are god-fearing travelers and men of sense, you will be advised by me: you will not rashly throw away your lives or rush into danger with the recklessness of youth. Make an experiment first. Send out a dove from *Argo* to explore the way. If she succeeds in flying between the Rocks and out across the sea, do not hesitate to follow in her path, but get a firm grip on your oars and cleave the water of the strait. For that is the time when salvation will depend, not on your prayers, but on your strength of arm. So think of nothing else, be firm, and spend your energies on what will pay you best. By all means pray to the gods, but choose an earlier moment. And if the dove flies on, but comes to grief midway, turn back. It is always better to submit to heaven; and you could not possibly escape a dreadful end. The Rocks would crush you, even if *Argo* were an iron ship. Ah, my poor friends, I do implore you not to disregard my counsel from the gods, even if you imagine their hatred of myself to be far more bitter than in fact it is. Do not dare to sail farther in, even if the bird's failure warns you to desist.

Gyllius identified two sets of Cyanean Rocks, one on either side of the Bosphorus at its mouth on the Black Sea. These two points, some 3,500 meters apart, are marked by beacons known as Rumelifeneri and Anadolufeneri, the Lighthouses of Europe and Asia, both of them surmounting fortified headlands that have fishing villages below them. The rocks on the European side more obviously match the description in *The Argonautica*. They are known in Turkish as Rokettaşları, a name that is probably derived from the French *roches* (rocks). They were originally about a hundred meters offshore from the fishing village of Rumelifeneri, but they have now been connected to the mainland by a concrete mole that forms part of the harbor. The rocks, which were about twenty meters high and divided into two parts by a deep fissure, now form part of a restaurant known as the Roket Lokantası. On the peak of the highest of the two rocks there are the remains of a monument known as the Column of Pompey. "The ascent to this peak," writes Gyllius, "is not open except by one approach, and this extremely narrow, so that one must climb up on all fours." The approach is just as difficult today, and should be made only by those who are agile and have no fear of heights. The award of intrepidity is a fine view of the Black Sea at the very mouth of the Bosphorus. The peak is still surmounted by the base of the ancient Column of Pompey. An engraving of the rock done in early Ottoman times shows the column still standing, its base bearing the inscription CAESAR in large Latin letters. The column was toppled by a storm in 1680 and had entirely disappeared by 1800. The column base is decorated with the carving of a garlanded ram's head and other reliefs, now much worn; it has traces of a Latin inscription, the correct transcription and interpretation of which is a matter of debate.

On a stormy day the huge waves rolling in from the Black Sea smash through the cleft in the Symplegades in great clouds of foaming spray, making it appear as if the rocks are indeed thunderously clashing together, at least if you use your imagination. This is the time to read the climactic passage in Book II of *The Argonautica*, where Apollonius describes how the helmsman Tiphys managed to get the *Argo* through, heeding the advice given by King Phineus, and with help at the crucial moment from Athena, who had been watching over the Argonauts in their time of peril:

Pompey's Column on the Clashing Rocks

10 FROM THE BOSPHORUS EASTWARD

In due course they found themselves entering the narrowest part of the winding strait. [Here and elsewhere the description by Apollonius reveals that he never sailed through the Bosphorus, which actually is widest at its mouth on the Black Sea.] Rugged cliffs hemmed them in on either side, and *Argo* as she advanced began to feel a swirling undercurrent. They moved ahead in fear, for now the clash of the colliding Rocks and the thunder of the surf on the shores fell ceaselessly on their ears. Euphemus seized the dove and climbed on the prow, while the oarsmen, at Tiphys' orders, made a special effort, hoping by their own strength of arm to drive *Argo* through the Rocks forthwith. They rounded a bend and saw a thing that no one ever after has seen - the Rocks were moving apart. Their hearts sank: but now Euphemus launched the dove on her flight and the eyes of all were raised to watch her as she passed between the Rocks.

Once more the Rocks met face to face with a resounding crash, flinging a great cloud of spray into the air. The sea gave a terrific roar and the broad sky rang again. Caverns underneath the crags bellowed as the sea came surging in. A great wave broke through the cliff and the foam swept high above them. *Argo* was swung around as the flood reached her.

But the dove got through, unscathed except for the tips of her tail-feathers, which were nipped off by the Rocks. The oarsmen gave a shout of triumph and Tiphys shouted at them to row with all their might, for the Rocks were opening again. So they rowed on full of dread, till the back-wash, overtaking them, thrust *Argo* in between the Rocks. Then the fears of all were turned to panic. Sheer destruction hung over their heads.

They had already reached a point where they could see the vast sea opening out on either side, when they were suddenly faced by a tremendous billow arched like an overhanging rock. They bent their heads down at the sight, for it seemed about to fall and overwhelm the ship. But Tiphys just in time checked her as she plunged forward and the great wave slid under her keel. Indeed it raised her stern so high in the air that she was carried clear of the Rocks. Euphemus ran along shouting to all his friends to put their backs into the rowing, and with answering shouts they struck the water. Yet for every foot that *Argo* made she lost two, though the oars bent like curved bows as the men put out their strength.

But now another overwhelming wave came crashing down on them, and when *Argo* had shot end-on like a rolling-pin through the hollow lap of this terrific sea, she found herself held back by the swirling tide just in the place where the rocks meet. To left and right they shook and rumbled; but *Argo* would not budge.

This was the moment when Athena intervened. Holding on to the hard rock with her left hand, she pushed the ship through with the other; and *Argo* clove the air like a winged arrow, though even so the Rocks, clashing in their accustomed way, sheared off the tip of the mascot on the stern. When the men had thus got through unhurt, Athena soared up to Olympus. But the Rocks were now rooted forever in one spot close to one another. It had been decided by the happy gods that this should be their fate when a human being had seen them and sailed through. The Argonauts, freed from the cold grip of panic, breathed again when they saw the sky once more and the vast ocean stretching out ahead. They felt that they had come through Hell alive.

Gyllius also identified a seagirt reef off the last promontory on the Anatolian shore of the Bosphorus as the Asian Symplegades. This point is known in Turkish as Yum Burnu, or Cape of Good Omen, the ancient Promentorium Ancyraeum. The ancient name means Cape of the Anchor, stemming from the legend that it was here that Jason took on a stone anchor for *The Argo*.

The road on the Asian side of the strait comes to an end at Anadolu Feneri. The road along the Asian shore of the Black Sea from there is open only to the military, so that civilian traffic must take a diversion inland via Alibahadır, from where a road leads out to the coast at Riva, the next seaside village east of Anadolu Feneri. Riva is at the mouth of the Riva Deresi, a river known in antiquity as the Rhebas. The village clusters around a ruined Genoese fortress dating from the early fourteenth century, which stands on the shore east of the mouth of the river. Apollonius mentions this river in his

12 FROM THE BOSPHORUS EASTWARD

description of the first stage of the voyage of the Argonauts along the coast of the Euxine, after they passed through the Clashing Rocks:

> ...they now devoted all their energies to rowing. Before long they passed the swift River Rhebas and the peak of Colone, and soon after that the Black Cape, and then the outfall of the River Phyllis. It was here that Phrixus son of Athamas had been entertained by Dipsacus when he was flying with his ram from the city of Orchomenus. This Dipsacus was the son of a meadow-nymph and the River Phyllis. He was an unassuming person who was quite content to live with his mother by his father's stream and graze his flocks by the sea. The Argonauts could see, as they passed them in turn, his shrine, and the broad banks of the river, and the plain, and the deep stream of Calpe; and all that day and through the windless night they labored at the indefatigable oar....

The other geographical features mentioned by Apollonius can still be identified along the coast beyond Riva. Colone is probably the promontory just to the north of Riva. The Black Cape, known in antiquity as Melaone Acra, can be identified with Karaburun, about five kilometers along the coast east of Riva, for the name has the same meaning in Turkish, Greek, and English. The rivers Calpe and Phyllis are, successively, farther to the east, but before coming to them we must make a detour inland from Riva. The detour takes us south via the villages of Göllü and Bozhane to highway 020, where we turn east for Şile, a drive of 36 kilometers.

As the road approaches Şile it passes the beautiful sand beach at Kumbaba, which stretches for miles westward towards the Bosphorus. The Kumbaba Motel is on the site of ancient Calpe, as evidenced by columns, capitals, and other architectural fragments that have been found and arrayed there. The stream that runs into the sea near the motel has been identified as the River Calpe mentioned by Apollonius. Calpe is mentioned by Xenophon in his *Anabasis*, an account of the epic journey that he and his comrades, the Greek mercenaries known as the Ten Thousand, made in the years 401-399 B.C. The Ten Thousand set out from Sardis in 401 B.C. in the service of Cyrus the Younger, who was attempting to usurp the throne of his elder brother, the Persian king, Artaxerxes II. Cyrus was killed at Cunaxa, north of Babylon, after which the Ten Thousand began their long march home, first heading north across Asia Minor to Trebizond, and then westward along the coast of the Euxine. The last stage of their journey along the Euxine brought them to Calpe, where they spent the winter of 400-399 B.C. While in Calpe they defeated a Bithynian force that attempted to dislodge them. Then the following spring they marched on and crossed the Bosphorus to Byzantium, where they were on the point of sacking the city before were given a subsidy to continue on their journey.

Şile was the harbor of ancient Calpe. Its setting is extremely picturesque, with the village perched on a cliff around a cove studded with half-a-dozen rocky islets, one of them surmounted by a ruined Genoese fortress of the fourteenth century. Xenophon describes the scene in his *Anabasis:*

> As for Calpe harbor, it...is a bit of land jutting out into the sea, the part of it which extends seaward being a precipitous mass of rock, and...[there is an] isthmus which connects this head to the mainland. The space to seaward of the isthmus is large enough to serve as a dwelling-place for ten thousand people. At the very foot of the rock there is a harbor whose beach faces toward the west, and an abundantly flowing stream of fresh water close to the shore....Our men took up quarters there on the beach by the sea....

Şile is noted for its cloth, a coarse cotton crêpe which the village women embroider in distinctive local designs. The cloth, which is used for making clothing, napkins, and tablecloths, is sold in shops along the main street of the village.

Eastward of Şile highway 020 winds up and down a valley before approaching the sea again at Ağva, where there is a beach

Gateway to the Genoese Fortress at Riva

with camping facilities at the mouth of a river. Ağva stands on the site of ancient Psillium. This place took its name from the fact that it stood at the mouth of the River Psillis, also known as the Phyllis, the form in which it is mentioned by Apollonius in *The Argonautica.*

After leaving Ağva we head westward on highway 41-03, continuing as far as the turn-off on the left for Kefken and Cebeci, two villages on the coast. Three kilometers beyond Kefken there is an excellent sand beach ending in a promontory with a tiny islet just to its west. The islet was known in antiquity as Thynias and the promontory as Apollonias, the latter so called because it was the

Ancient Tombstone from Calpe, at Kumbaba, Şile

site of a sanctuary of Apollo. After he has described the coast between Rhebas and Calpe, Apollonius writes of this islet in Book II of *The Argonautica* as follows:

> The crew of *Argo* all through the night ploughed the salt sea with their oars. But at the time of day when heavenly light has not yet come, nor is there utter darkness, but the faint glimmer of light that we call twilight spreads over the night and wakes us, they ran into the harbor of the lonely isle of Thynias and went ashore exhausted by their labors. Here they had a vision of Apollo on his way from Lycia to visit the remote and teeming peoples of the North. The golden locks streamed down on his cheeks in clusters as he moved; he had a silver bow in his left hand and a quiver slung on his back; the island quaked beneath his feet and the sea ran high on the shore. They were awestruck at the sight and no one dared to face the god and meet his lovely eyes. They stood there with bowed heads while he, aloof, passed

Genoese Fortress at Şile

through the air on his way across the sea.

Apollonius goes on to write of how the Argonauts, at the suggestion of Orpheus, dedicated an altar to Apollo on the islet, worshipping the god there before they continued on their voyage:

> Orpheus found his voice at last. "Come now," he said to the Argonauts, "let us dedicate this island to Apollo of the Dawn and call it by that name, since it was here that we all saw him pass by in the dawn. We will build an altar on the shore and make such offerings as we have at our command"....When the Argonauts had worshipped the god with dance and song, they made holy libations and touching the sacrifice as they spoke they took an oath to stand by one another in unity for ever. A temple of Concord can be seen on the spot to this very day....

We now return to highway 41-03 and resume our drive eastward, continuing along its extension, highway 54-77. As the road approaches the next large village, Karasu, it crosses the Sakarya Nehri, the ancient River Sangarius, twice mentioned by Homer in *The Iliad*. After passing through Karasu we continue straight ahead on highway 101, which, with a few deviations inland, runs eastward along the Black Sea coast all the way to the eastern border of Turkey. The next large village that we come to is Akçakoca, where the present itinerary comes to an end.

Tyche, the Goddess of Fortune

CHAPTER TWO

ISTANBUL TO AMASRA: EXCURSION TO SAFRANBOLU

Most travelers setting out from Istanbul on a journey along the Black Sea take the new superhighway as far as Düzce, turning off there to drive northward to the coast at Akçakoca, where the last itinerary ended.

The drive from Istanbul to Düzce, the ancient Dusae pros Olympium, takes one through the region known in antiquity as Bithynia, which extended eastward from the Bosphorus and the Propontis as far as Paphlagonia.

Bithynia was at the beginning of history inhabited by Thracians, who had crossed over the Bosphorus from their native Thrace. Herodotus mentions this in Book VII of his *History,* where he describes the Thracian troops in the army with which Xerxes invaded Greece in 480 B.C.:

> The Thracian troops wore fox skins as a headdress, tunics with the zeira, or long cloak, in this case highly colored, thrown over them, and high fawnskin boots; their weapons were the javelin, light shield and small dagger. The Thracians after their migration to Asia became known as the Bithynians; previously, according to their own account, they were called Strymonians, after the river Strymon upon which they lived, and from which they were driven by the Teucrians and Mysians. The commander of these Asiatic Thracians was Bassaces, the son of Artabanus.

During the fourth century B.C. the Thracians of Bithynia, who were constantly at war with the Greek coastal cities, formed a kingdom ruled successively by chieftains known as Foedalsus, Botiras, Bas, and Zipoetes. Zipoetes fought three successful campaigns resisting Lysimachus, one of the successors of Alexander the Great; and his third victory led him to assume the title of king of Bithynia in 297 B.C. In 280 B.C. he defeated the Seleucid king, Antiochus I; but he died shortly afterwards. Zipoetes was succeeded by his son Nicomedes I, who in 265 B.C. founded the city of Nicomedeia (İzmit) as the capital of Bithynia. Bithynia, which by that time was completely Hellenized, reached its greatest extent under his grandson, Prusias I (228-185 B.C.), who considerably expanded the boundaries of his kingdom along the shores of the Euxine and the Propontis, taking the Greek coastal settlements and founding new cities of his own. The boundaries of the kingdom remained essentially undiminished for more than a century after his reign, but then in 74 B.C. the history of Bithynia came to an end when its last king, Nicomedes IV (94-74 B.C.), bequeathed his realm to Rome.

We turn off the superhighway at the Düzce exit, taking highway 655 north for Akçakoca. A short way beyond the junction with highway 14-78 we take a turn-off on the right for Konuralp, which is just a few hundred meters from the main road.

Konuralp occupies the site of the ancient Bithynian city of Cierus, which was refounded by King Prusias I as Prusias ad Hypium. The latter part of the city's new name came from the fact that it stood on the River Hypius, distinguishing it from two other cities founded by Prusias at about the same time, namely Prusias ad Olympium (Bursa) and Prusias ad Mare (Gemlik). The remains of Prusias ad Hypium include stretches of its defense walls, a three-arched bridge, the theater, and a gateway, whose lintel bears the faint relief of a mounted warrior. The bridge and the theater both date from the first century A.D., but the walls and the gateway are Byzantine. The setting is extremely picturesque, for the ruins are in the center of a very attractive village, some of whose houses are built from fragments of the ancient city.

The local archaeological museum has an interesting and attractively displayed collection of antiquities from Prusias ad Hypium, including a Roman copy of the famous Venus de Milo, a statue of Aphrodite untying her sandal; a figure of Cybele, the Anatolian mother-goddess; a representation of an unidentified

Roman emperor; several sarcophagi with elaborate reliefs; and a large number of architectural fragments and inscriptions. The Istanbul Archaeological Museum has a colossal statue from Prusias ad Hypium: a figure of Tyche, the goddess of fortune, who is shown carrying a cornucopia, the "horn of plenty," which object symbolizes the fruits of the earth that she has bestowed on mankind. This fine sculpture dates from the Roman era.

We now continue along highway 655, which takes us through a verdant valley to the Black Sea coast, a drive of 36 kilometers from Düzce. We then turn left on highway 010, and after a drive of five kilometers we come to Akçakoca, an attractive resort village on a good sand beach.

Although Akçakoca has become a tourist resort it is still a typical village of the Black Sea coast, one that has preserved its distinctive Pontic characteristics despite the crowds of visitors who come here in the summer. Like the other villages of the Black Sea coast its principal products are hazelnuts (*fındık*) and anchovies (*hamsi*), the latter being a staple of the Pontic diet, used not only on its own but also as an ingredient for making bread, omelettes, and other foods. The various food products and traditional handicrafts of the region are on display during the Akçakoca Tourism and Nut Festival, which is held annually on the third Friday, Saturday, and Sunday of July and includes performances of local music and folk dances, as well as other cultural activities.

Akçakoca has been identified as the ancient Diapolis, of which nothing remains except a ruined Genoese fortress of the fourteenth century, located two kilometers to the west of the town. The lower course of the fortress walls appear to be Byzantine. The fortress and its immediate surroundings have been converted into a park. It is a place of great natural beauty, from which one has a superb view of the tree-clad coast to the west and its succession of promontories and coves. Three kilometers farther to the west is the mouth of the Melen Çayı, the ancient River Hypius. The Hypius is mentioned by Apollonius in Book II of *The Argonautica,* in a passage where King Lycus of the Mariandyni tells the Argonauts

Theater at Ancient Prusias ad Hypium, Konuralp

Ereğli, 1839, Print from Ainsworth

about the incursion of his neighbors, the savage tribe known as the Bebryces. "They have cut off large parcels of my land," he tells them, "thrusting their frontier right up to the meadows watered by the deep River Hypius."

We now turn back and begin driving eastward on highway 010. Some 22 kilometers beyond Akçakoca we come to Ereğli, a port town that is used principally for shipping coal. Ereğli also has the largest steelworks in Turkey. The town, which is built on terraces that run along the side of the hill above the harbor, is overlooked by the ruins of a Byzantine fortress.

Ereğli occupies the site of ancient Heracleia Pontica, founded ca. 560 B.C. by Greek colonists from Megara and Boeotia. Heracleia was the birthplace (ca. 400 B.C.) of Heraclides Ponticus, a student of Plato who headed the Academy during his master's absence in Sicily. Heraclides is renowned in the history of science for being the first to say that the earth rotated on its own axis and that the planets Mercury and Venus revolved around the sun.

In 368 B.C. Heracleia fell into the hands of the tyrant Clearchus, who made it the capital of a little kingdom that included four small cities to the east and substantial territory in the hinterland. When Clearchus died he was succeeded by his brother Satyrus and then in turn by his sons Timotheus and Dionysus. When Dionysus succeeded as tyrant he made a brilliant match with the Persian princess Amastris, a niece of Darius III whom Alexander had married off to Craterus, his second-in-command. When Craterus cast her off, Amastris married Dionysus; and when he died she inherited his kingdom. Amastris then married another of Alexander's generals, Lysimachus, after which she ruled as queen in a new city that she had founded in her own name—Amastris—farther eastward on the Pontic coast. Soon afterwards she was murdered by her two sons, Clearchus and Oxathres, who then took control of the kingdom. Lysimachus avenged her by killing the usurpers, replacing them with his new wife Arsinoë, daughter of Ptolemy I. After the death of Lysimachus in 280 B.C. the people of Heracleia revolted and established a democratic government, whereupon Arsinoë fled to

Egypt and four years later married her brother Ptolemy II, ruling as queen until her death in 270 B.C.

Heracleia was allied to Rome soon after 188 B.C. But in 74 B.C. it was forced to rebel against Roman rule by Mithridates VI Eupator, king of Pontus, who that year began the third and last of his wars against Rome. The city was recaptured by the Romans under Cotta, a lieutenant of Lucullus, who pillaged and burned it in reprisal. After the final defeat and death of Mithridates in 63 B.C. Heracleia was rebuilt and a Roman garrison was stationed there. Strabo, who would have first seen Heracleia soon after its return to Roman rule, gives a summary of its history in Book XII of his *Geography:*

Now Heracleia is a city that has good harbours and is otherwise worthy of note, since, among other things, it has also sent forth colonies; for both Chersonesus and Callatis are colonies from it. It was at first an autonomous city, and then for some time was ruled by tyrants, and then recovered its freedom, but later was ruled by kings, when it became subject to the Romans. The people received a colony of Romans, sharing with them a part of their city and territory. But Adiatorix, the son of Domnecleuis, tetrarch of the Galatians, received from Antony that part of the city which was occupied by the Heracleiotae; and a little before the Battle of Actium he attacked the Romans by night and slaughtered them, by permission of Antony, as he alleged. But after the victory at Actium he was led in triumph and slain together with his son. The city belongs to the Pontic Province which was united with Bithynia.

Heracleia became a bishopric in the third century A.D. As its bishopric is older than that of Constantinople, the Bishop of Heracleia has always preceded the Bishop of Constantinople in ecclesiastical processions. The city remained part of the Byzantine Empire until the capture of Constantinople by the Latins in 1204. A fragment of the Byzantine Empire survived under the Comnenian dynasty in Trebizond, known as the Empire of Trabizond. This Comnenian state continued in existence after Constantinople was recaptured in 1261 by the Greeks under Michael VIII Palaeologus. Its first ruler was Alexius Comnenus, whose brother David took Heracleia Pontica in 1205 and made it the capital of his domain. The Genoese established a commercial colony in Heracleia in 1261, and then in 1360 they bought the city from the declining Empire of Trebizond. The city was taken by the Ottomans soon after their capture of Constantinople in 1453. Its present name of Ereğli derives from its Greek name.

The principal remnants of Heracleia Pontica are its defence walls and citadel, which date from the Byzantine period. Incorporated in these walls are some architectural fragments of the ancient city. This is evident from a description by Ainsworth, who visited Ereğli in 1839:

> The present town occupies only the south-west corner of the space covered by the ancient city, and contains 250 houses of the Mohammedans and 40 houses of Greek Christians. The walls of the town extend along the sea-shore, then ascend a hill which they divide in half up to its highest point, where they encircle the ruins of an acropolis, having a Greek inscription of the Byzantine era in front. The wall then returns along the side of the valley called Tabena Derehsi, which has a small rivulet at its centre. The walls are in a ruinous condition, and constructed in part from the fragments of older ramparts. There occur in them numerous fragments of columns, stones with crosses, cornices, tablets with Greek inscriptions, showing that they were erected in the Byzantine era.
>
> In that part of the wall which fronts the sea there are the remains of another and outer wall, which is chiefly composed of vast irregular masses of basalt, and limestone cemented by mortar. This wall contains no fragments of Byzantine architecture. It probably defended the city anterior to that period, and the encroachment of the sea necessitated that, when rebuilt it should be farther inland. Connected to the last outer wall are the remains of a long and crude mole, which advances from its northern end into the sea....The valley of the brook appears to have been a harbour for galleys, and there are still the remains of towers which defended it.

Ereğli has grown considerably since Ainsworth's time, and the modern town now completely covers the site of the ancient city. There are still substantial remains of Heracleia Pontica to be seen; a study published in 1965 by Professor Wolfram Hoepfner contains a map showing sixty-two sites. These sites include the Byzantine citadel; the city walls, sections of which date from the Hellenistic, Roman, and Byzantine periods; an aqueduct; a street; a mole; two Byzantine churches converted to mosques; two mosques and two houses that contain architectural or sculptural fragments; a Byzantine cistern; an unidentified Byzantine ruin; and a number of other ancient remains and inscribed fragments. One of the Byzantine churches, now known as the Orta Cami (the Middle Mosque), has been dated to the reign of Theodosius II (408-50); it is a basilica with its nave separated from the side aisles by two colonnades of marble columns with ancient Ionic capitals.

Excavations have also made on the north side of the town into three grottoes that have since antiquity believed to be entrances to the Cave of Heracles, also known as the Cavern of Hades. Travelers always describe this cavern to be near the promontory now known as Baba Burnu, the ancient Promentorium Acherusias, which forms the northern arm of Ereğli's harbor. The cavern was thought to be one of the entrances to the underground torrent Acheron, one of the rivers of Hades along with the Styx; and it was believed that this was where Heracles made his way into the Underworld to bring back the dog Cerberus, the hound of Hell. The excavations have revealed that the three grottoes were part of a cave sanctuary known as the Acherontal, which was apparently sacred to Hecate, goddess of the night and of the underworld, as evidenced by the discovery there of several reliefs and a statue representing her and her cult. The excavations also revealed that the shrine of Hecate was converted into a Christian sanctuary in the fifth or sixth century.

The Promentarium Acherusias and the Cave of Hades are mentioned by Apollonius in Book II of *The Argonautica*, where he describes the voyage of the Argonauts from the isle of Thynias to their landing in what is now the harbor of Ereğli:

With dawn on the third day there came a fresh west wind, and they left the lofty island. Skirting the mainland coast, they saw in turn the mouth of the River Sangarius, the fertile lands of the Mariandyni, the River Lycus and the Anthemoeisian lagoon. The ship's halyards and all the other tackle quivered in the wind as they sped along; but during the night the breeze dropped, and with thankful hearts they made harbour at dawn by the Cape of Acherusias. This lofty headland, with its sheer cliffs, looks out across the Bithynian Sea. Beneath it at sea level lies a solid platform of smooth rock on which the rollers break and roar, while high up on the very summit plane trees spread out their branches. On the landward side it falls away into a hollow glen. Here is the Cavern of Hades with its overhanging trees and rocks, from the chill depths of which an icy breath comes up and every morning covers everything with sparkling rime that melts under the midday sun. The frowning headland is never visited by silence; a murmur from the sounding sea mingles for ever with the rustling of the leaves as they are shaken by the winds from Hades' Cave.

The so-called Cave of Heracles is still pointed out on the northeast side of Ereğli. Xenophon mentions this cave in his account of the last stages of the journey of the Ten Thousand along the coast of the Euxine, referring to the eleventh of the twelve labors of Heracles. In his account Xenophon puts it as follows:

And coursing along they arrived at Heracleia, a Greek city and a colony of the Megarians, situated in the territory of the Mariandynians. And they came to anchor alongside the Acherusian Chersonese, where Heracles is said to have descended to Hades after the dog Cerberus, at a spot where they now show the marks of his descent, reaching to a depth of more than two stadia. Here the Heracleots sent to the Greeks, as gifts of hospitality, three thousand medimni of barley meal, two thousand jars of wine, twenty cattle and a hundred sheep.

Apollonius continues his account of the *Argo*'s landfall at the Acherusian Cape:

> Here too is the mouth of the River Acheron, which issues from the mountain-side and falls, by way of a deep ravine, into the eastern sea. On a later occasion the Megarians of Nisaea, when on their way to settle in the land of the Mariandyni, had good reason to call this river the Sailor's Saviour: the harbour at its mouth saved them and their ships when they were caught in a violent gale. The Argonauts brought their ship to the same spot. Shortly after the wind had dropped, they beached her in the shelter of the Acherusian Cape.

The Argonauts were greeted by King Lycus of the Mariandyni. The Mariandyni treated Jason and his shipmates with great honor because they had eliminated their enemy Amycus, king of the Bebyrces, who had been killed by the Argonaut Polydeuces in single combat. But during their stay two of the Argonauts were killed, first the soothsayer Idmon, son of Abas, and then the helmsman, Tiphys. The Argonauts buried Idmon and Tiphys in turn; and then, after choosing Ancaeus as their new helmsman, they set sail once again. In his description of the next stage of their voyage, Appollonius recounts some momentous episodes that had taken place in the past along that stretch of the coast, most notably the expedition of Heracles against the amazons, the legendary women warriors who were believed to inhabit this region.

> At dawn on the twelfth day a fresh breeze was blowing from the west. So they went on board, rowed swiftly out from the mouth of the Acheron, and then set their sail to the wind and forged ahead through clear weather under a broad spread of canvas. They soon came to the mouths of the River Callichorus, where we are told that Dionysus Son of Zeus, when he had left the Indians and was on his way to Thebes, established revels, with dances in front of a cave, in which he himself passed holy and unsmiling nights. Ever since then, the people of the place have called the stream the River of the Lovely Dance, and the

Cave the Bedchamber.

Next day they saw the tomb of Sthenelus son of Actor, who had joined Heracles in his daring attack on the Amazons, and on the way ·back had died on the beach from an arrow wound. They paused here, for the goddess Persephone sent up to them the mourning ghost of Actor's son, who craved to see some men of his own kind, if only for a moment. He stood on the edge of his barrow and gazed at the ship, appearing to them in his warlike panoply, with the lights flashing from the four plates and purple crest of the fine helmet that he used to wear. Then he sank down again into the great abyss. The Argonauts were awestruck at the sight, and Mopsus, speaking as their seer, told them to land and with libations lay the ghost. So they quickly sailed the sea, cast hawsers on the shore, and paid honour to the tomb of Sthenelus. They made libations to him and sacrificed some sheep as offerings to the dead. Then, in a separate place, they built an altar to Apollo, Saver of Ships, and burnt the thigh-bones of the sheep. Orpheus made an offering of his own. He dedicated a lyre, in memory of which the place is still called Lyra.

Highway 010 heads inland for a way to skirt around Baba Burnu. It then returns to the coast for only a short stretch before it comes to Zonguldak, the main port for Turkey's largest coal-mining region. Zonguldak is on the site of ancient Sandarace, of which not a trace remains. There is nothing of note to see in Zonguldak except the very lively port, which harbors many old vessels of the Black Sea coasting trade.

We continue along the coast east of Zonguldak on highway 67-01, passing the village of Çatalgazi. There are three remarkable caves in the vicinity of Çatalgazi: Cumayanı Mağarası, Gökgöl Mağarası, and Çayırköy Mağarası, all of which are open to tourists.

Highway 67-01 brings us along the coast as far as Hisarönü. Hisarönü stands on the site of ancient Tieum, where Miletus founded a colony in the seventh century B.C. The village is on a projecting headland, with a harbor protected by moles made from so-called cyclopean masonry, the huge stone blocks of prehistoric date that the

Greeks attributed to the mythical giants that they called the cyclopes. Tieum was one of the four smaller cities that formed part of the kingdom created by Clearchus, the tyrant of Heracleia Pontica. Philetaerus, the founder of the Attalid dynasty of Pergamum, was born in Tieum ca. 343 B.C. Aside from the moles of its harbor, the only remnants of ancient Tieum in Hisarönü are fragments of its theater and a temple, along with a fairly well-preserved medieval fortress.

Hisarönü is a short distance to the west of the Yenice Irmağı, the River Billaeus of antiquity. Beyond Hisarönü the road turns inland and brings us south along the Yenice Irmağı to Çaycuma, where we turn eastward to cross the river, after which we drive three kilometers to rejoin highway 010 and turn left for Amasra. Some 16 kilometers before Amasra the road passes Bartın, the ancient Parthenios, a lively village that contains many old Ottoman houses. The village is situated on the Bartın Çayı, known in antiquity as the River Parthenios. The river and the ancient city were named for the virgin (Greek *parthenos*) goddess Artemis, who bathed in its waters, according to local legend. This is a matter of some importance in the identification of the various ancient cities along this coast, since five of them are mentioned in *The Iliad,* along with the river.

The River Parthenios here formed the boundary between Bithynia and Paphlagonia, which was bounded on the east and the southeast by the Halys River. The River Parthenios is mentioned in Book II of *The Iliad,* where Homer lists the Paphlagonians among the Asian contingents who fought as allies of King Priam of Troy.

> Pylaimenes the wild heart was leader of the Paphlagones,
> from the land of the Enetoi where the wild mules are engendered,
> those who held Kytoros and those who dwelt about Sesamos,
> those whose renowned homes were about the Parthenios river,
> and Kromna and Aigialos and high Erythinoi,...

A drive of 15 kilometers beyond Bartın brings us out to the sea again at Amasra, our route following the course of an ancient Roman road. The last stretch of the road winds down through a series of hairpin turns with sweeping views of the coast and of the medieval walls of Amasra.

Amasra takes its name from the ancient city of Amastris, on the site of which it stands. Pliny the Younger, who was governor of the Roman province of Bithynia ca. A.D. 110, in the reign of Trajan, describes Amastris as *"a handsome and well equipped city."* The setting of Amasra is typical of that of an ancient Greek coastal city, built on a seagirt promontory connected to the mainland by a narrow isthmus, with deeply indented harbors on both sides. There was a citadel on the promontory and a defense wall across the isthmus, where the city's two main gates were located.

The original name of the city was Sesamos, a colony founded by Miletus in the sixth century B.C. But there must have been a settlement here before this time, for Sesamos is one of the places hereabouts mentioned by Homer in *The Iliad.* When Queen Amastris came to power she renamed Sesamos after herself, refounding it as

Ruins of Ancient Teium, Hisarönü

the capital of her Pontic kingdom. After she was murdered by her sons, Lysimachus took control of the city of Amastris, appointing as his governor Eumenes of Tieum, a brother of Philetaerus, whom he had left in charge of his treasury at Pergamum. After the death of Lysimachus in 281 B.C. Philetaerus took control of Pergamum, and two years later Eumenes took refuge with him there, having surrendered Amastris to Ariobarzanes, king of Pontus. After the Pontic kingdom came to an end Amastris was made capital of the Roman province of Bithynia-Pontus. It remained under Byzantine control until 1398, when it was taken over by the Genoese, who held it until they surrendered it to the Ottomans in 1461.

The picturesque ruins of the citadel and part of the defense walls survive, along with a watchtower on a tongue of rock that juts out into the harbor, linked to the mainland by a Roman bridge. The walls we see today are all of Byzantine construction; but they are probably built on Hellenistic foundations, this being one of the oldest cities on the coast. Besides these there are also the remains of the gateway to the theater and the ruins of a gymnasium-baths complex known locally as the Bedesten. The local museum has antiquities found in the town and its environs, including several Roman tombstones and the numerous fragments of a colossal temple, possibly dedicated to Poseidon. There are also three Byzantine churches that were converted into mosques in the Ottoman era, now known as Fatih Camii, Kilise Mescidi, and Büyükada Manastırı. The only relics of the Genoese presence are a number of coats-of-arms in the citadel, including one belonging to Duke Visconti of Milan, who ruled over Genoa in the years 1421-36.

Before continuing eastward along the coast one might make a detour inland to the south via Bartın to visit Safranbolu, a drive of 91 kilometers that goes over the Ahmetusta Pass. This is a pass with an altitude of 1,580 meters.

Safranbolu is famous for its old Ottoman houses; and it is the only town in Turkey that has preserved almost all of its traditional dwellings, a restoration project that began in 1975. One of these houses is the Havuzlu Konak (a *konak* is a town house or mansion),

Amasra

Amasra, the Acropolis

dated 1822, which has been converted into a hotel by the Turkish
Touring and Automobile Club. The oldest of the dated houses was
erected in 1787, and eighteen others are known to have been built
in the nineteenth century. All of these and many other venerable
dwellings of undetermined date have been superbly restored, along
with their carved and painted woodwork and ceilings with intricate
inlaid designs, some of the rooms still preserving their original
painted decoration. Among the other distinguished old houses (*ev*)
that have been restored in the town are the Emirhocazade Ahmet
Bey Evi, Hacı Salih Paşa Evi, Kavsalar Evi, Memişoğulları Evi,
Hacıhüseyinlerin Evi, Karaosmanların Evi, Kaymakamlar Evi, and
Paşacıoğlu Evi. Craftsmen still work at their traditional trades in
the Arasta, the old bazaar street, and tradesmen do business in the
old-fashioned way in shops that have not changed in their appearance
since late Ottoman times.

Aside from the village houses, Safranbolu has three monuments
from the Beylik period and more than forty from the Ottoman,
including ten mosques (*cami*), a theological school (*medrese*), a

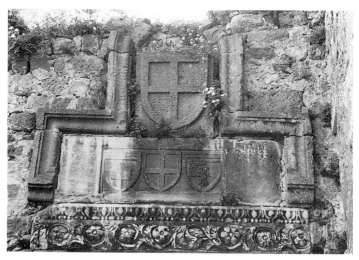

Amasra, Genoese Coats-of-Arms in Fortress

Amasra, Fishing Boats under the Sea Walls

caravansarai (*kervansaray*), two public baths (*hamam*), a dervish lodge (*tekke*), four tombs (*türbe*), and twenty-one fountains (*çeşme*). Aside from the fountains, the dated monuments include the following: Eski Cami (ca. 1322), Eski Hamam (ca. 1322), Gazi Süleyman Paşa Medresesi (ca. 1322), Kalealtı Tekkesi Camii, (1550), Cinci Hoca Kervansarayı (1640), Köprülü Mehmet Paşa Camii (1662), Hidayetullah Camii (1719), Dağdelen Camii (1768), Kazdağlı Camii (1779), İzzet Mehmet Paşa Camii (1796), Ali Baba Tekkesi (1824), Hasan Baba Türbesi (1845), Hacı Emin Efendi Türbesi (1867), Şeyh Mustafa Efendi Türbesi (1871), Ali ve Hasan Baba Türbeleri (1872), Kaçak Camii (1879), and Hamidiye Camii (1884).

After visiting Safranbolu we retrace our route to Amasra. En route we can rest our eyes on the splendid prospect of the Küre Dağları, the mountain chain that rises above the Black Sea coast of Paphlagonia. Hamilton's description of this magnificent mountain scenery, written more than one hundred and fifty years ago, is still true today, with virtually nothing of the modern world intruding on the wild beauty of the Pontic landscape:

Safranbolu, View of the Town

Old Ottoman House in Safranbolu

For the first mile the country was open and undulating, with few patches of cultivation, and large clumps of wood on all the neighbouring hills. A mile and a half from the village we descended into a deep ravine extending nearly east and west, where the contrast between the two sides in point of vegetation was very remarkable; that to the south facing the north being covered with firs, wild pears, beech and hornbeam, all clothed with a profusion of thin, long, pendent, hoary moss, while that to the north was perfectly bare. A little farther on the valley was joined by another from the S.W., which we ascended, while the united streams flowed together towards the N.N.W., apparently falling into the Chobanlar Chai [Shepherds' River]. The valley which we now entered was thickly wooded, the fir and beech trees had attained a considerable size, and some of the latter were truly magnificent; but the woods were cold and damp, and even the beeches, instead of presenting as usual a smooth and shining bark, were covered with a long hoary lichen. As we advanced the scenery became wilder and more alpine; the mountains stretching far away to the east and west, and wooded to their very summits, still bore those extensive forests, for which, under the name of Peucia Silva, the shores of the Black Sea were celebrated in antiquity, and through the uncleared and undisturbed labyrinths of which we were now following a wild and rarely trodden path....

CHAPTER THREE

AMASRA TO SİNOP:
EXCURSION TO KASTAMONU

Our next itinerary will take us eastward along the coast from Amasra to Sinop via İnebolu, where we will take an excursion south across the mountains to Kastamonu.

The first part of our excursion will take us from Amasra to Cide, a drive of 78 kilometers. This will take us past the other four ancient places mentioned in *The Iliad* along with Sesamos—"Kytoros...and Kromna and Aigialos and high Erythinoi"—all of which have been identified. In order of their location from Amasra eastward: Erythinoi is at Çakraz, Kromna at Kurucaşile, Kytoros at Gideros, and Aigialos at Cide, where there is an immensely long sand beach that extends all the way past Kerempe Burnu, the Cape Carambis of antiquity. The identification of all four places is based on inscriptions, but otherwise there is nothing to be seen at any of them except the remains of a medieval fortress at Gideros, which preserves in corrupted form the ancient name of the site. Cide also has an Ottoman mosque founded in the third quarter of the seventeenth century by Merzifonlu Kara Mustafa Paşa, grand vezier under Mehmet IV. All of these places and another called Crobialos are mentioned by Apollonius in Book II of *The Argonautica,* where he describes the voyage of the Argonauts after Orpheus had made an offering at the place called Lyra:

When this was done, as the wind was blowing hard, they re-embarked, let down the sail and drew it taut with both sheets. And *Argo* sped eagerly over the sea, like a high-flying hawk that has set its pinions to the breeze, and flapping them no more glides on swiftly across the sunny sky with wings at rest. They were soon past the spot where the Parthenios flows out to the sea; a gentle river this, in whose delectable waters Artemis refreshes herself before ascending to heaven after the

chase. Then they pressed on in the night without a stop, passing
Sesamos and the crests of Erythinoi, Crobialos, Kromna and wooded
Kytoros. At sunrise they rounded Cape Karambis, and all that day and
on through the night they rowed *Argo* along the endless shore of
Aigialos.

A winding, up-and-down drive of 96 kilometers from Cide brings
us to İnebolu, the next large town along the coast. İnebolu stands
on the site of ancient Abonuteichus, a Greek colony founded in the
sixth century B.C. by Sinope. During the reign of Marcus Aurelius
(161-80) it came to be known as Ionopolis, from which the Turkish
name İnebolu is derived. Strabo describes Abonuteichus as "a small
town." Nevertheless in the mid-second century A.D. it won
considerable renown as the home of Alexander of Abonuteichus, a
charlatan who became famous throughout the Roman world as an
oracle and healer who founded a mystical sect that was particularly
popular among women. He was condemned and reviled by the
satirist Lucian, who referred to him as "the False Prophet of
Abonuteichus." All that remains of Ionopolis are the fragmentary
ruins of its citadel, along with an inscribed statue base, which stands
at the crossroads where Ömer Kaptan Sokağı joins the shore road
on the western bank of the İnebolu Çayı.

At İnebolu we will make an excursion south over the mountains
to Kastamonu, a drive of 88 kilometers. The road winds up from
the coast in a series of hairpin turns and after a drive of 22 kilometers
it brings us to Küre, where the Ulu Cami, or Great Mosque, dates
from the fifteenth century. We then go over a series of passes all
exceeding 1,200 meters in altitude and finally come to Kastamonu.
The town lies on both sides of a narrow valley formed by a minor
tributary of the upper Gökırmak, its old Ottoman houses and Islamic
monuments clustering around a great rocky acropolis surmounted
by the ruins of a medieval fortress.

Kastamonu is probably of great antiquity, as evidenced by its
early Paphlagonian rock tombs; but nothing is known of its history
prior to the medieval era. The town was taken by the Selçuk Turks

soon after their great victory over the Byzantines at the battle of Manzikert in 1071. Subsequently it was held in turn by the Byzantines, Selçuks, Ilkhanid Mongols, three Turkmen *beylik*s, or principalities— the Çobanoğulları, the Çandaroğulları, and the İsfendiyaroğulları— and then the Ottomans. The Ottomans lost the town for a time after Beyazit I was defeated by Tamerlane at the battle of Ankara in 1402, but then it was recaptured by Mehmet II in 1462.

The only Byzantine monument in Kastamonu is the medieval fortress on the acropolis, which was rebuilt in the Turkish era. The town is richly endowed with Islamic monuments from the Selçuk, Beylik and Ottoman periods, including 55 mosques and mosque complexes (*külliye*), 66 tombs, 26 theological schools and libraries (*kütüphane*), 16 public baths, 10 large commercial buildings (*han*), 42 fountains, including a *şadırvan,* or mosque ablution fountain, one covered market (*bedesten*), and one bridge (*köprü*). The earliest of the mosque complexes is the Yılanlı Külliyesi, founded in 1272 as a hospital (*darüşşifa*) and orphanage (*darüşşafaka*) with a small mosque (*mescit*), approached by a monumental stone portal in the Selçuk style. The oldest of the mosques is Atabey Gazi Camii, built in 1273 by an emir (Atabey) of the Çobanoğulları (Sons of the Shepherd) who was awarded the title of Gazi, or Warrior for the Faith and who is buried in a semicylindrical *türbe* within the complex. Some of the other mosques and mosque complexes of the Selçuk, Beylik and Ottoman periods are Akçasu Camii (thirteenth century), İbni Neccar Camii (1353), Abdürrezzak Camii (1389), Honsalar Camii (1417), İsfendiyar Bey Camii (1439), İbrahim Bey Camii (1443), Hamza Ağa Camii (1446), Deveci Sultan Camii (1450), İsmail Bey Külliyesi (1443-61), Musa Fakih Camii (1466), Şeyh Şabanıveli Külliyesi (1490-1500), Nasrullah Kadı Külliyesi (1506), Benli Sultan Külliyesi (1512-20), Rüştem Paşa Camii (1530), Yakup Ağa Külliyesi (1547), Ferhat Paşa Camii (1559), Sinan Bey Camii (1571), Saray Camii (1575), Hasan Efendi Camii (1588), Hacı Dede Camii (1591), Ahmet Dede Camii (1600), Aycılar Camii (1674), Hepkebirler Camii (1675), Halife Sultan Camii (1675), Küpceğiz Camii (1675), Server Camii (1675), Cebrail Camii (1689),

Tabaklar Camii (1689), Alamescit Camii (1715), Abdülcebbar Camii (1748), Hasan Çelebi Camii (1767), Alparslan Camii (1769), Safalan Camii (1786), Molla Said Camii (1814), Ovalı Pazarı Camii (1850), Kazancılar Camii (1872), Baha Efendi Camii (1885), and Cevkanı Camii (1892).

The other Islamic monuments of Kastamonu include Şeyh Ahmet Türbesi (1206), Abdülfettahıveli Türbesi (1210), Nasrullah Köprüsü (1230), Atabeygazi Medresesi (1250), Frenkşah Hamamı (1262), Müfessir Alaeddin Efendi Türbesi (1289), Ahi Ali Baba Türbesi (1300), Süleyman Paşa ve İbrahim Bey Türbesi (1320-41), İbrahim Paşa Medresesi (1341), İbni Neccar Türbesi (1353), Adil Bey Türbesi (1345-61), Süleyman Bey Türbesi (1368), Mehmet Bey Türbesi (1370), İsa Dede Türbesi (1400), Selçuk Hanım Türbesi (1429), Hatun Sultan Türbesi (1436), İsfendiyar Bey Medresesi (1439), İsmail Bey Hanı (1460), Kale Hamamı (1460), Cem Sultan Bedesteni (1469), Balkapan Hanı (1481-1512), Kanlı Çeşme (1510), Sarının Hanı (1512), Abdürrezzak Türbesi (1513), Çifte Hamamı (1514), Dede Sultan Hamamı (1514), Beyçelebi Medresesi (1523), Bayraklı Dede Türbesi (1533), Hisarardı Hamamı (1557), Acem Hanı (1571), Ferhat Paşa Hamamı (1557-74), Saray Hamamı (1575), Ahmet Dede Türbesi (1631), Numaniye Medresesi (1688), Bey Hamamı (1689), Topçuoğlu Şadırvanı (1727), Yanık Han (1730), Atlanbaç Çeşmesi (1744), Abdülcebbar Türbesi (1748), Aşir Efendi Hanı (1748), Taş Çeşme (1761), Şekerci Ali Bey Çeşmesi (1770), Tarakçılar Çeşmesi (1766), Saray Çeşmesi (1772), Safalan Çeşmesi (1786), İsmail Bey Çeşmesi (1798), Kancı Çeşmesi (1800), Kara Mustafa Paşa Medresesi (1811), Yeni Hamam (1811), Münire Medresesi (1824), Tevfikiye Medresesi (1824), Namazgâh Medresesi (1868), Sıdkıyye Medresesi (1877), and Halidiye Kütüphanesi (1878).

There are two ancient Paphylagonian rock-hewn tombs in Kastamonu, one of them near İsmail Bey Camii and the other near the Endüstri Meslek Lisesi, both of them dated ca. 700 B.C. Other ancient remains are exhibited in the local Archaeological Museum, which also has an ethnographical collection as well as Atatürk memorabilia.

There are two early mosques in the environs of Kastamonu. One of these is in the village of Kasaba, 15 kilometers northwest of Kastamonu. This is Mahmut Bey Camii, a wooden mosque erected in 1366 by a son of the Çandaroğulları emir Adil Bey. This is one of only four wooden mosques in Turkey that date from the pre-Ottoman period, and it retains all of its original carved woodwork and painted decoration, beautifully preserved in a recent restoration.

The second mosque is in the village of Duruçay 12 kilometers north of Kastamonu on the İnebolu highway. This is Halil Bey Camii, erected in 1363 by Halil Bey bin İsmail, a Çandaroğulları emir. The most interesting features of this mosque are the two re-used Byzantine Ionic capitals that crown the marble columns in its porch, both of them delicately carved.

We now return to İnebolu and resume driving eastward along highway 010. The first large village that we pass is Abana, some 25 kilometers beyond İnebolu. The place appears to be of considerable antiquity, as evidenced by the architectural fragments of the Graeco-Roman and early Byzantine periods found in the village, but no suggestions have been made concerning the identity of the site, although its Turkish name obviously derives from Abonuteichus.

Some 16 kilometers farther along we come to Ginolu. The village stands on the classic site of an ancient Greek city, a seagirt promontory with harbors on either side. This has been identified as the site of ancient Kinolis, whose name is preserved in only slightly corrupted form in that of the village and the nearby ruined fortress known as Ginolu Kalesi, which is apparently of Byzantine construction.

About ten kilometers beyond Ginolu we pass Güllüsu Kalesi, another ruined Byzantine fortress. This is all that remains of ancient Colussae, although the word Colussae can still be discerned in its Turkish form of Gülüsu.

At Halaldı the highway curves inland and then cuts back to the coast again at Ayancık. We then drive along the shore as far as Incirpinar, where the highway leads inland again to cross the base of the huge peninsula just to the west of Sinop. This is İnceburun,

known in antiquity as the Promentorium Syrias, the northernmost
point on the coast of Asia Minor. This promontory is mentioned by
Apollonius in Book II of *The Argonautica,* though under a slightly
different name, for he refers to it as "the Assyrian coast." Here he
refers to the myth of the nymph Sinope, who became the eponymous
founder of the Greek city of the same name; and he also mentions
the legend of Heracles and his battle against the amazons who were
believed to live along this coast. As he writes, after describing how
the Argonauts "rowed *Argo* along the endless shores of Aegialus
(Aigialos):"

> They landed on the Assyrian coast, where Zeus himself had once given a
> home to Sinope, daughter of Asopus, granting her the boon of virginity.
> He was trapped by his own promise. In his passion for the girl he had
> solemnly sworn to fulfill her dearest wish, whatever that might be; and
> she very cleverly had said, "I wish to remain a virgin." By the same ruse
> she outwitted Apollo when he made love to her; and the River-god
> Halys as well. Men fared no better than the gods; this woman never was
> possessed by any lover.
>
> On the coast here, Deileon, Autolycus, and Phlogus (sons of the
> admirable Deimachus of Tricca) had been living ever since they lost
> touch with Heracles. When they saw the party land from *Argo* and
> observed their rank, they approached them, told them who they were and
> expressed a wish to leave the place for good. They were taken on board
> at once, as the North-West Wind brooked no delay; and the Argonauts,
> with these recruits, were carried along by the fresh breeze, leaving behind
> them the River Halys, its neighbour the Iris, and the delta-land of Assyria.
> It was here that Melanippe daughter of Ares, having sallied out one day,
> was caught in an ambush by the great Heracles, though he let her go
> unharmed when her sister Hippolyte gave him her own resplendent girdle
> by way of ransom. And here in the bay beyond the cape, as the sea was
> getting rough, the Argonauts ran ashore at the mouth of the Thermodon.

Strabo in Book XII of his *Geography* explains why the word
"Syrian," and by extension "Assyrian," was used as a toponym

here, just westward of the point where the River Halys empties into the Euxine. In the following passage he wites of Themiscra, the supposed home of the amazons, in the valley of the Thermodon above the Euxine coast:

> As for the Paphlagonians, they are bounded on the east by the Halys River, "which," according to Herodotus, "flows from the south between the Syrians and the Paphlagonians and empties into the Euxine Sea, as it is called," by "Syrians," however he means the "Cappadocians," and in fact they are still today called "White Syrians," while those outside the Taurus are called "Syrians." As compared with those this side the Taurus, those outside have a tanned complexion, while those this side do not, and for this reason received the appellation "white," and Pindar says that the Amazons "swayed a 'Syrian' army that reached afar with their spears," thus clearly indicating that their abode was in Themiscra. Themiscra is in the territory of the Amiseni; and this territory belongs to the White Syrians, who live in the country next after the Halys River.

The Promentorium Syrias actually has two headlands, of which the western one was known as Lepti Akri, "the fine cape," while the eastern one was called Armene. The eastern cape was in antiquity the site of a settlement called Armene. Apparently it was very small, as Strabo infers from his description of the coast just westward of Sinop: "...Armene, to which pertains the proverb, 'whoever had no work to do walled Armene'. It is a village of the Sinopeans and has a harbor." Xenophon and the Ten Thousand stopped in this little harbor, then known as Harmene, pausing before they rounded the Promentarium Syrias on their homeward journey. We pass to the south of the cove, now known as Akliman, as we come within sight of Sinop, the ancient Sinope. Strabo describes the city as it was in his time, some two thousand years ago, first giving a resume of its history:

> Then one comes to Sinope itself, which is fifty stadia [about ten km] from Armene; it is the most noteworthy of the cities in that part of the

world. The city was founded by the Milesians; and having built a naval station, it reigned over the sea inside the Cyaneae [the Cyanean Rocks at the entrance to the Bosphorus on the Black Sea], and shared with the Greeks in many struggles even outside the Cyaneae; and although it was independent for a long time, it could not eventually preserve its freedom, but was captured by siege, and was first enslaved by Pharnaces [Pharnaces I of Pontus] and afterwards by his successors down to Eupator [Mithridates VI] and to the Romans who overthrew Eupator. Eupator was both born and reared at Sinope; and he accorded it special honour and treated it as the metropolis of his kingdom. Sinope is beautifully equipped both by nature and by human foresight, for it is situated on the neck of a peninsula, and has on either side of the isthmus harbours and roadsteads and wonderful palamydes fisheries... Higher up...and above the city, the ground is fertile and there are diversified market-gardens, especially in the suburbs of the city. The city is beautifully walled, and is also splendidly adorned with gymnasium and market-place and colonnades. But although it was such a city, it was twice captured, first by Pharnaces, who unexpectedly attacked it all of a sudden, and later by Lucullus and by the tyrant who was garrisoned within it, being besieged both inside and outside at the same time; for since Bacchides, who had been set up by the king as commander of the garrison, was always suspecting treason from the people inside, and was causing many outrages and murders, he made the people who were unable either nobly to defend themselves or to submit by compromise, lose all heart for either course. At any rate, the city was captured, and though Lucullus kept intact the rest of the city's adornments, he took away the globe of Billarus and the work of Sthenis, the statue of Autolycus, whom they regarded as founder of the city and honoured as god. The city had also an oracle of Autolycus. He is thought to have been one of those who went on the voyage with Jason and to have taken possession of this place. Then later the Milesians, seeing the natural advantages of the place and the weakness of the inhabitants, appropriated it to themselves and sent forth colonists to it. But at present it has received also a colony of Romans; and a part of the city and the territory belong to these....It has also produced excellent men: among the philosophers Diogenes the Cynic and Timotheus Patrion; Diphilus the comic poet, and among the historians Baton, who wrote the work entitled the *Persica.*

Diogenes (404 - 323 B.C.), son of Hicesius of Sinope, is renowned as the founder of the Cynic school of philosophy in Athens. He led an exceedingly simple life, living in a tub within the sanctuary of the Metroön in Athens and the other temples and stoas of the Agora, as Diogenes Laertius describes him doing in his *Lives of the Eminent Philosophers:*

Through watching a mouse running about, says Theophrastus in the *Megarian Dialogue,* not looking for a place to lie down in, not afraid of the dark, not seeking any of the things which are considered to be dainties, he discovered the means of adapting himself to circumstances. He was the first, some say, to fold his cloak because he was obliged to sleep in it as well, and he carried a wallet to hold his victuals, and he used any place for any purpose, for breakfasting, sleeping or conversing. And then he would say, pointing to the portico of Zeus and the Hall of Processions, that the Athenians had provided him with places to live in... he took for his abode the tub in the Metroön, as he himself explains in his letters. And in summer he used to roll in it over hot sand, while in winter he used to embrace statues covered with snow, using every means of inuring himself to hardship.

He was great at pouring scorn on his contemporaries. The school of Euclides he called bilious, and Plato's lectures waste of time, the performances at the Dionysia great peep shows for fools, and the demagogues the mob's lacqueys. He used also to say that when he saw physicians, philosophers and pilots at their work, he deemed man the most intelligent of all animals; but when again he saw interpreters of dreams and diviners and those who attended them, or those who were puffed up with wealth, he thought no animal more silly....

Alexander is supposed to have said, "Had I not been Alexander, I should have liked to be Diogenes...." When he [Diogenes] was sunning himself in the Craneum, Alexander came and stood over him and said,

"Ask any boon you like." To which he replied, "Stand out of my light."

Archaeological explorations have revealed 39 prehistoric sites in the vicinity of Sinop, the earliest dating back to 4,500 B.C. The city of Sinope was founded as a Greek colony by Ionian settlers from Miletus in the seventh century B.C. The Sinopeans soon afterwards established daughter colonies along the Euxine shore eastward of their own city at Cotyora (Ordu), Cerasous (Giresun), and Trebizond (Trabzon), all of them paying tribute to their mother city. Sinope soon became the leading port in the Euxine, controlling trade among the Greek colonies on the coast of both Anatolia and the Crimea.

Sinope also established a little empire of its own, comprising three enclaves along the Euxine coast of Anatolia. The first and largest enclave extended from Sinope eastward to the River Halys, where it met the lands of its neighbor Amisus (Samsun); the second was from Cape Jason to the Sinopean daughter colonies of Cotyora and Cerasous; and the third was from Coralla (Görele) eastward to Trebizond.

Sinope retained its independence until 183 B.C., when the city and its little empire were taken by Pharnaces I of Pontus. Because of its importance as a port Sinope soon replaced Amaseia (Amasya) as capital of the Pontus and the burial place of the Pontic kings. The Pontic kingdom reached its peak under Mithridates VI Eupator ("the Great"), who was born in Sinope in 135 B.C. When Mithridates came to the throne in 120 B.C. he fortified the city, building the powerful citadel and defence walls that still survive in part today. He fought the Romans in three widespread conflicts that came to be known as the Mithridatic Wars, the first of which began in 88 B.C. and the last ending with his defeat and death twenty-five years later. His opponent in the third and last of these wars was Lucullus, who captured Sinope in 67 B.C. Four years later, after the final defeat and death of Mithridates by Pompey, the Romans annexed Sinope and established a colony there. Sinope continued to be the leading port in the Euxine, retaining its status as a free city under

Sinop, View from Fortress Window

the aegis of Rome for another four centuries.

During the Byzantine era Sinope continued to be the principal port in the Euxine, its position at the narrowest part of the Black Sea giving it control of the maritime trade between Asia Minor and the Crimea. After the Latin conquest of Constantinople in 1204 Sinope fell into the hands of Alexius I Comnenus of Trebizond, but ten years later the city was taken by the Selçuk Turks under Sultan İzzeddin Keykavus. The city was recaptured ca. 1255 by Manuel I Comnenus of Trebizond, but in 1265 it fell to the Selçuk emir Muinettin Süleyman, known as the Pervane. Thenceforth it remained in Turkish hands more or less permanently, although in the years 1298-1324 the Comneni of Trebizond and their Genoese allies made repeated attempts to retake the city, which by then was called Sinop. Then in 1324 it came under the control of the İsfendiyaroğulları emirs, who at that time ruled Paphlagonia from their capital at Kastamonu. When Kastamonu fell to the Ottomans under Beyazit I in 1391 the İsfendiyaroğulları made Sinop their capital, holding it

Sinop, Walls and Towers of the Fortress

until Mehmet II conquered Paphlagonia and the Pontus in 1461. Sinop suffered enemy attacks twice during the Ottoman period, first in 1614 by Cossack raiders, and then on 30 November 1853 by the Russian Navy, the latter incident triggering the Crimean War.

Hamilton first arrived in Sinop on 23 July 1836; and though he remained for only three days, he explored the town and its environs in minute detail. Having arrived at the town as one does today, along the narrow isthmus that connects it to the mainland, he describes his entry into Sinop which occurred just after seven in the evening:

The narrow isthmus was covered with fine sand blown up by the prevailing north-west winds. On this side Sinope is defended by a strong wall, apparently Byzantine, which stretches from N.W. to S.E., and which is strengthened by several towers, some of which have skewed considerably from the perpendicular. We entered the outer gate of the town by a narrow winding passage through the wall, and then passed eastwards, between the citadel on our right, and the sea wall on the left, to the inner gate. We rode quickly through the streets, and issuing again on the east side, soon found ourselves in the Greek quarter, where the governor had assigned me a *konak*. The place is said to contain 500 Turkish houses within the walls, and 300 Greek houses, all outside, and chiefly to the east of the town.

It was with feelings of the greatest satisfaction that I at length found myself within the walls of this celebrated city, once the capital of the kingdom of Mithridates Eupator, by whom it was embellished, and who also formed a harbour on each side of the narrow isthmus; a city no less illustrious in its origin, than in its defence against hostile attacks, and in its final fall; and remarkable as the birth-place of the cynic philosopher Diogenes. Its modern name is Sinab; but nothing remains standing of its once celebrated buildings, its magnificent halls, and the beautiful temples, with which it was embellished by successive princes and rulers; the few traces of its former magnificence, which I subsequently found in rambling about the town and neighbourhood

Mithridates VI Eupator, King of Pontus, Bronze Miniature in the British Museum

during the three days I remained there, will be described in the following pages.

Hamilton began his exploration of the town the following morning after calling on the *bey*, or lord, the title held by the governor.

Quitting the Bey's apartment, I proceeded to explore the town and ruined walls in search of antiquities and inscriptions....Near the eastern gate the whole of the wall across the isthmus on this side has been built up with fragments of ancient architecture, such as columns, architraves, etc., and I promised myself a rich harvest of inscriptions. The same profusion of ancient fragments existed in the court-yard of a mosque near the centre of the town, where they were arranged on each side of the different paths and avenues leading to a large fountain. In many of the principal streets fragments of architraves and columns are seen in the foundations of houses; and the outer wall to the west is also formed of similar remains....All appeared to have belonged to edifices erected by or in honour of the Emperor Germanicus. A large marble lion is also worked into the same-wall towards the south....

I then proceeded to visit the citadel, or Utch Kaleh, as it is called, which extends across the isthmus to the west of town. These walls are composed of ancient fragments, proving the complete destruction of former buildings. Outside the gate, on the circular pedestal of a statue which had been hollowed out, and converted into a mortar for grinding or bruising wheat, is an inscription in honour of Antonine, the son of Antoninus Pius....The inner portion of the wall on the west side of the citadel is raised upon arches, supported by piers of very beautiful construction, which appear Roman, and are probably the remains of an aqueduct....The second or outer wall, which extends across the isthmus, is built of old materials, and is probably the work of Byzantines or Genoese. Being raised upon sand, some of the towers have fallen from the perpendicular, and still present a grotesque appearance, more recent fortifications having been built upon them. From the tower at the S.W. angle I could trace the ancient mole, by which the port was formerly defended, extending under water in an irregular line the whole length of the city, leaving a narrow entrance for small vessels, which is even now the only entrance to the harbour.

The citadel is inhabited by Turkish families and contains nearly fifty houses. Crossing the town to the north I passed through a sally-port, and descended to the beach....In a tanner's yard near this entrance were several sarcophagi, used as troughs, on one of which was a short inscription.

In the evening I proceeded to the east end of town, to visit what was called the ruins of a temple, a short way up the hill. They belonged to an old Byzantine church built of alternate layers of brick and stone. Within it was a modern Greek church almost entirely under ground, with a few broken columns lying near....On the slope of the hill to the east of the town are substructures and vaults built with Roman bricks, and the ground about is strewed with fragments of pottery and tiles. One building particularly attracted my attention; it consisted of three large vaulted chambers, which, from the incrustation, probably formed a cistern.

The population and prosperity of Sinope are not such as might be expected in a place offering such a safe harbour between Constantinople and Trebizond. I observed also a general appearance of poverty and privation throughout the peninsula. Many Roman and Byzantine coins were brought me, and a few silver of Sinope, some of Amisus, and a beautiful silver one of Kromma; but the occasional arrival of the steamer, and the consequent increase of communication with the capital, had taught the owners to ask large prices.

Sinop has increased considerably in size since Hamilton's time, though the Greeks here and elsewhere in Anatolia have now gone, deported in the exhange of minorities that followed the Graeco-Turkish war of 1919-22. The prosperity of Sinop has significantly increased as well, particularly in the last quarter of a century, as it has in all of the towns along the Black Sea coast. This increased growth and prosperity have resulted in the destruction of part of the ancient walls of Sinope, particularly because of the widening of the main road leading into the town, so that only two of the gateways are still standing, Kumkapı and Loncakapı. Nevertheless, the walls are still a most impressive sight, some three kilometers in length, with a thickness of eight meters and standing to a height of 25-30 meters, 43 of the original 60 towers surviving at least in part. The lower courses of the defenses date back to the pre-Mithridatic age, but the upper parts have been rebuilt by all of the various powers who have held the city in turn. These walls originally surrounded the isthmus that connected the mainland with the seagirt promontory now known as Boztepe, the Gray Hill. The acropolis and citadel were just inside the line of walls that cut off the neck of the isthmus at its narrowest stretch, where it is less than 400 meters wide. The city's main harbor was just to the south of this isthmus, protected by a mole that can still be seen submerged there; besides this there was a second port on the north side of the isthmus.

Other than the defense walls, the most impressive ancient structure that has survived is Balatlar (Palaces), so called because of the belief that this was the palace of Mithridates. This enormous building complex, whose scattered ruins cover an area of some 10,000 square meters, is about 300 meters southeast of the city walls on the lower slope of Boztepe. There are 15 different chambers in the complex, the largest of them measuring about 18 by 40 meters. One of these is known as Balat Kilisesi, "Palace Church," which has extensive areas of wall paintings, some of them fairly well preserved. The paintings have been dated to 1640 by an inscription, which records the dedication of the church to the Dormition of the Virgin.

The Archaeological Museum is in the center of Sinop, just to the east of the innermost wall in the defense circuit of the ancient city. The exhibits include finds from the prehistoric sites in the vicinity of Sinop, as well as objects found in the city itself, ranging in date through the archaic, classical, Hellenistic, Roman, Byzantine, Selçuk and Ottoman periods. There is also an ethnographical section that features objects that were used in the daily life of Sinopeans in the Ottoman era, including the colorful local folk costumes, as well as a collection of icons from the town's former Greek Orthodox churches.

Among the objects in the museum garden are architectural fragments of the Serapeum, excavated on this site in 1951 by Professors Ekrem Akurgal and Ludwig Budde. The temple was rectangular in plan, measuring 8.60 by 15 meters, with an altar on the south side. The excavators found figures of Serapis, Isis, Dionysus, Heracles and Persephone, as well as pottery and architectural fragments. Two inscriptions indicate that the temple was dedicated to Serapis, and other evidence has dated it to the fourth century B.C. According to Tacitus, the cult of Serapis originated in this temple, spreading from here to Egypt during the reign of Ptolemy I (305-282 B.C.).

Also in the garden of the museum is a Turkish war memorial, honoring the Turkish sailors who were killed when the Russians attacked Sinop in 1853.

The oldest Islamic monument in Sinop is Alaattin Camii, built soon after the Selçuk conquest of the city in 1214 and subsequently restored on several occasions. The second oldest is the Alaattin Medresesi, founded in 1262 by Muinettin Süleyman, the Pervane. Other Islamic monuments are Fatih Baba Mescidi (1353), Saray Camii (1374), Cezayirli Ali Paşa Camii and Seyyit Bilal Camii, the latter two being works of the Selçuk period mentioned by the Arab traveller Ibn Battuta, who visited Sinop in 1332. There are also a number of Islamic tombs dating from the early Turkish period, including the Seyyit Bilal Türbesi, Hatunlar Türbesi, Yeşil Türbe, İsfendiyaroğulları Türbesi, and Sultan Hatun Türbesi, the latter built for a sister of the Ottoman sultan Murat I (1359-89).

Within a chamber of the Alaattin Medresesi there is a *türbe* with a stone sarcophagus bearing the following inscription: "This is the tomb of Gazi Çelebi, son of Masud." Gazi Çelebi, who may be a great grandson of the Pervane, ruled Sinop as Emir of the İsfendiyaroğulları in the years 1298-1324; and during that time he carried on almost continual warfare with the Comneni of Trebizond and their Genoese allies. After the Comneni gave the Genoese a base in Trebizond in 1319, Gazi Çelebi attacked the city and burned down part of it. The Greeks and Italians retaliated by sending a fleet in a surprise attack on Sinop, but their expedition met with disaster, as İbn Battuta relates, writing of the extraordinary courage of Gazi Çelebi, who would seem to have been the first frogman known to history:

> This Gazi Çelebi was a brave and audacious man, endowed by God with a special gift of endurance under water and power of swimming. He used to make expeditions in war galleys to fight the Greeks, and when the fleets met and were fighting he would dive under water, carrying in his hand an iron tool with which to hole the enemy's galleys, and they would know nothing of what had befallen them until the foundering of their ships took them unawares. On one occasion a fleet made a surprise attack on the harbor and he holed them and captured all the men who were on board. He possessed indeed a talent that was unmatched, but they relate that he used to consume an excessive quantity of hashish...

CHAPTER FOUR

SİNOP TO SAMSUN:
EXCURSION TO AMASYA

Our next itinerary will take us eastward along the coast from Sinop to Samsun, with an excursion south across the mountains to Amasya.

The first stage of our journey will take us from Sinop to Gerze, a drive of 32 kilometers. Hamilton, who rode along this coast in approaching Sinop, describes the verdant scene as follows.

> For some time the road was excellent; hedges of bay and myrtle served to protect the gardens and orchards on both sides of the road, after which we emerged on a wild open country, with a few scattered trees; we then crossed a small stream, flowing N.E., and again entered a well-cultivated district, where the fields, also enclosed with hedges, were teeming with crops nearly ripe. Nowhere in Asia Minor had I seen a country so English in its appearance, or so like one of our own rich arable counties. Sinope too appeared to great advantage over the deep blue sea.

Gerze has been identified as ancient Karousa. Virtually nothing remains of the ancient town, which is thus described by Hamilton:

> Gherseh, anc. Carusa, contains about 240 houses, all of which, except about 25 Greek, are Turkish....I strolled about the place for some time, and visited the narrow point which forms the harbour, where there is a ruined wooden fort with six brass guns. Passing through the town I saw what had once been the pedestal of a statue, but without an inscription; in the wall of an old Byzantine church, however I found one fragment, as well as another in a Greek church close by, in the courtyard of which were two Corinthian capitals and several broken columns. These were all the evidences of antiquity I could discover....the description of the harbour, as given by the anonymous

Funerary Relief from Amisus, Samsun Museum

Periplus [an ancient navigator who described the coast of the Euxine] is quite appropriate..."a good port when the wind blows from the west," which is the case. Arrian merely says that it is a bad station for ships.

Twenty-three kilometers beyond Gerze we come to Kerim, a seaside village backed by precipitous cliffs at the mouth of the stream known as the Aksu Çayı. Hamilton identified this site as the site of ancient Zagora, describing the setting as he approached the village from the west:

This portion of the road was exceedingly bad, being only a narrow path between the perpendicular cliff and the blue waves, over huge masses which had been precipitated from above, and where we were obliged alternately to enter the water to avoid the rocks, and to scramble over the rocks to avoid the deep water, to the great distress of the horses and the injury of the baggage. At a quarter after eleven we left

Mouth of Aksu Çayı, Print from Hamilton

the beach, and crossing a low ridge of hills suddenly came in sight of the Chai Ak Su, the mouth of which was immediately below us, entering the sea between the ridge on which we stood, and a rocky hill to the west.

Descending from the hill, our road led some way up the thickly-wooded valley, watered by this river, which we crossed and recrossed several times. The plane-trees, which grew luxuriantly at the bottom, were large and flourishing....After following the river some way towards the west, we turned north, and ascended, through oak and fir trees, the steep hill running from east to west, and separating the valley from the sea, and to avoid which we had been compelled to leave the sea-shore. Its almost perpendicular sides must once have rendered it a place of great security, and likely to have attracted attention in former days. There can be little doubt that it was the site of Zagora, which Arrian places at 150 stadia from Carusa—the same distance as from Carusa to Sinope; and on measuring the coastline on the map I find exactly fifteen geographical miles....This proportion of ten stadia to a geographical mile....I have generally found more available in the application of comparative geography than any other....

Twenty-one kilometers farther along we come to Alaçam. Hamilton identified this as the site of ancient Zalecus, which after the reign of Leo I (457-74) was named Leontopolis in his honour. Virtually nothing is left of the ancient town, and today one looks in vain for even the few fragmentary ruins mentioned by Hamilton in the following description of Alaçam and its eastern approaches:

After leaving the cafe we passed for several miles through a rich and well-enclosed country, abounding in hedgerows, while numerous streams from the hills varied the scene to our dusty eyes, and gave a sure promise of abundant crops. The hills on the left were well wooded; at half-past two we entered a narrow and well-watered valley to the south, and in about half a mile reached the village of Alatcham. On the banks of the small stream, as well as near the entrance of the valley, were some of the finest plane-trees I had anywhere seen, but their tops were mostly gone—broken off or injured by time and weather. I measured the girth of several at about three feet from the ground, where the diameter was least, and found that one was thirty-five feet, and others above thirty feet in circumference.

The house which was assigned to me for my lodging had such a filthy and uncomfortable look, and the dry green grass before it, near the river, was so tempting, that I determined to have my tent pitched for the first time, and found it most cool and delightful: while the servants were preparing it I wandered up the valley to the ruins of an old castle or fortress, about a mile from the village, on the summit of a pointed and wooded hill. I reached it with some trouble, after scrambling through thickets and briars, but found nothing to reward the toil. The view towards the north, however, was picturesque; and as I descended by another road to the village, I unexpectedly met with, on a lower hill, the ruins of a more considerable building, but so completely buried in the woods, and overgrown by shrubs, that it was impossible to have any idea of its plan or extent. The solid walls, which are built of alternate layers of stone and bricks, like those of Constantinople, appeared to belong to the Byzantine period, but I saw neither doors nor windows. The situation of the valley and ruins corresponds with that of the river and town of Zalecus....

We continue on another 26 kilometers to Bafra. As we approach the town we cross the Kızılırmak, the River Halys of antiquity, which here marks the boundary between Paphlagonia and the Pontus. Hamilton describes the scene:

About a mile from Bafra we reached the banks of the Kizil Irmak, flowing from S.W. to N.E. in two narrow beds about 300 yards apart from each other. The first branch we crossed by a long wooden bridge; the second we forded: in the rainy seasons, however, the mass of water must be very great, for the stony bed of the river was above a quarter of a mile in width. The colour of the water was precisely that of the Tiber, more yellow than red, which is the real meaning of the word kızıl....For some distance the road led through natural orchards of apple and other fruit trees, and various creepers. The apples, though not quite ripe, were perfectly sweet; on crossing the Halys we had entered Paphlagonia, which even in the time of the Romans was celebrated for its apples....

Ancient Paurae may have been on the banks of the Halys east of the present town of Bafra. There are two prehistoric habitation mounds near the river crossing; and these probably mark the original site of Paurae, which continued in existence until at least the late Byzantine period. The Princess Anna Comnena, writing in *The Alexiad,* records that Raymond of St. Giles and other leaders of the First Crusade escaped by ship from Paurae in 1101, after their army was defeated by the Selçuks at the battle of Phazimon (Merzifon).

Soon after crossing the second branch of the river we enter the town of Bafra. The town has long been famous for its tobacco, which is collected here from the surounding area and shipped off to Istanbul, where it is used in the making of cigarettes. In the passage that follows, one that concerns his visit to the town of Bafra, Hamilton mentions tobacco:

Soon after four we descended into the plain of Bafra, and as we approached the town passed several chiftliks [farms] and cottages in the plain, which became more frequent as we advanced. Near the town the ground was marshy, and we entered the place by a long and narrow causeway. It had a clean and quiet look, embosomed in gardens and trees, with nothing but the tall minaret of the mosque to announce that we were approaching a town of so much consequence. I was informed by the Greek papas [priest], whose residence I found prepared for my reception, that it contains 1160 houses, of which 1000 are Turkish, 100 or 110 Greek, and 50 Armenian....The crowded streets announced that it was bazaar or market day, and the road by which I left the town was thronged with peasants, many of whom were driving small carts laden with tobacco, the produce of the surrounding districts....

The mosque mentioned by Hamilton is Büyük Cami, founded in the mid-seventeenth century by Ayşe Hatun, wife of Köprülü Mehmet Paşa, who was grand vizier under Mehmet IV.

After leaving Bafra we cross the eastern half of the great promontory formed by the delta of the Kızılırmak. This region was known in antiquity as Gazilonitis, as Strabo notes in his description of the Euxine coast immediately to the east of the Halys delta.

After the outlet of the Halys comes Gazelonitis, which extends to Saramene; it is a fertile country and is everywhere level and productive of everything. It has also a sheep-industry, that of raising flocks clothed in skins and yielding soft wool, of which there is a great scarcity throughout the whole of Cappadocia and Pontus. The country also produces gazelles, of which there is a scarcity elsewhere....

The road comes out to the sea again at Dereköy, the ancient Konopeion, and from there a drive of some 30 kilometers along the shore brings us to Samsun.

Samsun, the ancient Amisus, is situated on a huge bay bounded by two enormous deltas, with the Kızılırmak on the west and on the east the Yeşilırmak, the River Iris of antiquity. The site of the ancient city is a large flat-topped acropolis hill called Kara Samsun, which projects into the sea north-northwest of the modern city. The hill is now occupied by the Turkish army and is thus off-limits to the public. Hamilton seems to have been the only traveler to have explored the site of ancient Amisus, of which he writes thus:

I started early with a Greek guide to visit the ruins of Amisus, Eski [Old] Samsun, as they are called by the Turks, on a promontory about a mile and a half N. N. W. from Samsun. On the eastern side of this promontory, called Kailou Bournu, is a low sandy marsh, on which stands a modern fort. This was once part of the harbour of Samsun, but the greater portion of it is now converted into gardens. From its N. E. extremity the pier which defined the ancient harbour may be distinctly traced, running out about 300 yards to the S. E., but chiefly under water. It consists of large blocks of a volcanic conglomerate, some of which measure nineteen feet by six or eight, and two feet in thickness; whilst a little farther north another wall extends E. N. E. to a natural reef of rocks....On the summit of the hill, where once stood the Acropolis, are many remains of walls of rubble and mortar, and the whole ground is strewed with fragments of Roman tiles, and within, and at a little distance to the S. E. are the remains of a square building with a round tower at one corner, apparently of Byzantine construction, with Roman tiles mixed up in it. The extent and direction of the ancient mole are very visible from this elevation. Near the south end of the brow of the hill overlooking the harbour I at length discovered traces of the real Hellenic walls; they are not extensive, but it is impossible to mistake their peculiar structure; and at the foot of the hill are the ruins of a small church, formerly dedicated to St. Theodore, but since converted into a mosque, the foundations of which consist of large blocks of stone, derived from the ruins of Amisus.

Amisus was founded ca. 564 B.C. by Ionian Greeks, probably from Miletus and Phocaea. A century later the colony was reinforced by an expedition of Athenians, who renamed it Piraeus after the port of Athens, though eventually the original name of Amisus came back into use. The harbor of Amisus was not as good as that of Sinope, but it had better access to the Pontic hinterland. Consequently it handled the bulk of overland commerce and eventually surpassed Sinope as a center of trade. Amisus had much the same history as Sinope in the Hellenistic era, reaching its peak during the reign of Mithridates VI Eupator, who adorned it with temples and other edifices. But in 71 B.C. a Roman army under Lucullus trapped Mithridates here and burned the city to the ground, the king barely escaping with his life. Lucullus was filled with remorse for having destroyed an ancient Greek city, and so he gave orders for Amisus to be rebuilt and for its surviving citizens to be rehoused on the site. The city soon recovered, and for the next fifteen centuries it was the leading port in the Euxine.

The city, which was known to the Turks as Samsun, was taken

by the Selçuks ca. 1194, after which it was captured in turn by the Comneni of Trebizond, the Selçuks again, the Ilkhanid Mongols, the İsfendiyaroğulları of Kastamonu, the Ottomans, and the İsfendiyaroğulları. In 1425 it became a permanent part of the Ottoman Empire. During the latter period of the İsfendiyaroğulları rule the Genoese established a trading colony in the city, which they called Simisso; and they seem to have built a fortress within gunshot of the Turkish citadel, as remarked by several travelers. The Arab chronicler Arapşah, after a visit in 1400, writes that at Samsun "a fort on the shore of the sea of the Mussulmans, was set opposite a like fort of the wicked Christians, which two are less than a stone's throw apart and each fears the other."

When the Ottomans finally took Samsun in 1425, the Genoese set fire to their quarter before they fled by sea, leaving the town a smoking ruin. The damage was not repaired, and Samsun was reduced to humble circumstances throughout most of the Ottoman period. As late as the 1860s it consisted of a Turkish village on the shore and a Greek hamlet at what is now the village of Kadıköy, their combined population less than 5,000. But then the completion of the Istanbul-Baghdad railroad in the late nineteenth century, with a branch from Ankara to Samsun, revived the town's trade, allowing it to export the tobacco for which it is now famous. By 1910 Samsun's population had grown to 40,000, and since then its numbers have increased to more than a quarter of a million, as it has become the most important port and commercial center on the Black Sea coast of Turkey.

Samsun gained prominence when Atatürk landed here on 19 May 1919 for a week's stay, during which time he began organizing the nationalist movement that would lead to Turkish independence. This historic occasion is commemorated by a monument in the main square and by two museums: the Atatürk Museum and the 19 May Museum. Samsun also has an archaeological museum with an ethnological collection. Some of the antiquities in the archaeological museum are from ancient Amisus, most notably mosaic pavements found on Kara Samsun, the acropolis-hill of the ancient city. The

oldest Turkish monuments are Pazar Camii, a mosque built by the
Ilkhanid Mongols in the thirteenth century, and an Ottoman mosque
erected in 1503. Otherwise Samsun is a completely new city, with
little evidence that it has a history stretching back more than twenty-
six centuries.

At Samsun we will take an excursion south on highway 795 to
Amasya, a drive of 127 kilometers. After going over the Hacılar
Pass, at an altitude of 670 meters, we pass the village of Çakallı. A
few kilometers farther along we pass the Çakallı Han, a ruined
Selçuk caravansarai dating from ca. 1240. During the days of the
Sultanate of Rum the Selçuks built caravansarais such as this along
all of the highroads of Anatolia, where travelling merchants could
stay free of charge for three days. More than fifty of these
caravansarais survive, most of them more or less in ruins, monuments
to the greatness of the Turkish empire that flourished in Anatolia
just before the rise of the Ottomans.

We then go over the Karadağ Pass, at an altitude of 950 meters,
after which we come to Havza. Then, 28 kilometers beyond Havza,
we come to Amasya, the ancient Amaseia, set at an altitude of 382
meters on the Yeşilırmak. The appearance of this beautiful and
historic town is best described by Hamilton, whose account is still
largely valid despite the ravages of unsightly modern building:

> The valley soon widened into a plain, when we came in sight of the
> Castle and Acropolis of Amasia, situated on the summit of a lofty
> rock on the opposite side of the river, the banks of which were fringed
> with gardens, wherever its waters could be raised for the purposes of
> irrigation. At half-past five we entered the town, winding through the
> narrow streets, admiring the remarkable caves in the rocks on the
> opposite side of the river, immediately under the castle, which are
> doubtless the tombs of the kings described by Strabo. Several Saracenic
> buildings, either in ruins or used as mosques, line the principal street
> through which we passed; many of the houses are built of stone,
> which, combined with its picturesque situation, give the town a great
> superiority over most others in Turkey. The population is said to

consist of 3000 to 4000 Turkish houses, 750 Armenian, and 100 or 150 Greek.

I remained three days at Amasia, but a much longer time might be well employed in examining the antiquities of the town and castle, in exploring the interesting localities in the neighbourhood, and in visiting the silver, copper and salt mines near Marsuvan. In Amasia itself the objects most worthy of notice are the Acropolis, the ancient walls, and the tombs of the kings; but perhaps the town derives its greatest interest from being the birthplace of Strabo, whose account is so clear and satisfactory that I shall venture to introduce it here before describing the present state of the city.

Strabo, the renowned Greek geographer of the Roman world, was born in Amaseia in 64 B.C. He left his birthplace to study at Nysa in western Asia Minor, going from there to continue his studies in Rome in 44 B.C. and later also in Alexandria. After completing his studies he travelled throughout the *oecumenos,* the

View of Amasya, 1836, Print from Hamilton

"known world," which he describes in detail in the seventeen books of his *Geography,* the only one of his works that has survived. His description of Amaseia is in Book XII, one of four volumes that he devotes to Asia Minor. He writes as follows:

> My city is situated in a large deep valley, through which flows the Iris River. Both by human foresight and by nature it is an admirably devised city, since it can at the same time afford the advantage of both a city and a fortress; for it is a high and precipitous rock, which descends abruptly to the river, and has on one side the wall on the edge of the river where the city is settled and on the other the wall that runs up on either side to the peaks. These peaks are two in number, are united with one another by nature, and are magnificently towered. Within this circuit are both the palaces and monuments of the kings. The peaks are connected by a neck which is altogether narrow, and is five or six stadia in height on either side as one goes up from the river-banks and the suburbs; and from the neck to the peaks there remains another ascent of one stadium [approximately 200 meters], which is sharp and superior to any kind of force. The rock also has reservoirs of water inside it, a water-supply of which the city cannot be deprived, since two tube-like channels have been hewn out, one towards the river and the other towards the neck. And two bridges have been built over the river, one from the city to the suburbs and the other from the suburbs to the outside territory; for it is at this bridge that the mountain which lies above the rock terminates. And there is a valley extending from the river which at first is not altogether wide, but it later widens out and forms the plain called Chiliocomun [the Thousand Villages]; and then comes the Diacopene and Pimolisene country, all of which is fertile, extending to the Halys River.

Amaseia became the first capital of the kingdom of Pontus under Mithridates I Ktistis, who reigned in the period 302-266 B.C. The greatest of the Pontic kings was Mithridates VI Eupator, who moved his capital from Amaseia to Sinope after he came to power in 120 B.C. After the death of Mithridates VI his son Pharnaces II attempted to regain his father's dominions by going to war against the Romans in 48 B.C., defeating an army led by Calvinus, Caesar's lieutenant. But the following year Caesar utterly defeated him at Zela, and soon afterwards Pharnaces was killed in a rebellion by his own people. This did not immediately end the kingdom of the Pontus, which was revived for a time by the Romans as a puppet state. "Afterwards," writes Strabo, "the Roman leaders made various divisions, setting up kings and dynasts, and leaving others under the rule of the Roman people." After Caesar made various changes, appointing and deposing local dynasts and altering provincial boundaries, Antony revived the Pontic Kingdom in 40 B.C., appointing as its ruler Darius, son of Pharnaces and grandson of Mithridates. A few years later the kingdom passed to Polemon I, and on his death in 8 B.C. he was succeeded by his widow, Queen Pythadoris. Pythadoris ruled until her death some time after A.D. 17, after which the long history of the kingdom of the Pontus comes to an end.

After the end of the Pontic Kingdom, Amaseia was at first part of the combined province of Galatia-Cappadocia, and then in the reorganization of Asia Minor under Diocletian it became part of the province of Diospontus. During the Byzantine period it was included in the province of Armeniakon. The city fell to the Arabs under the Caliph Walid I in 712, but it was recaptured soon afterwards by the Byzantines under Leo III. After the Selçuks defeated the Byzantines at the battle of Manzikert in 1071, Amaseia fell to the Türkmen tribe known as the Danışmendid who made it the capital of their emirate under the name of Amasya. Amasya was then ruled in turn by the Selçuks, the Mongols, the Eretnid emirate, and then in 1391 it was taken by the Ottomans under Beyazit I. Amasya was a provincial capital under the Ottomans, and a number of future sultans served as military governors before succeeding to the throne, among them Mehmet I (ruled 1413-21), Murat II (1421-51), Mehmet II (1451-81), and Beyazit II (1481-1512). As a result, Amasya is richly endowed with Islamic monuments from the earliest Turkish periods up through Ottoman times.

Most of the monuments of Amasya are on the right bank of the

Yeşilırmak, which within the town is crossed by six bridges, one of them, the Çağlayan Köprüsü, dating back to the twelfth century. We might begin our tour along the main avenue at the western end of the town on the right bank of the Yeşilırmak, on the road to Tokat, making our way eastward, crossing the various bridges in turn to see the monuments on the other side of the river.

The first monument we come to, on our right as we walk back into the center of town along the main avenue, is Gökmedrese Camii. This is a Selçuk mosque that also served as a *medrese*, with a *türbe* attached to its left side and another larger free-standing tomb in front of it. An inscription identifies the founder as the Emir Şerafettin Torumtay, a slave of the Selçuk sultan Keykubad II who became Governor of Amasya. The mosque and its attached *türbe* were built in 1266/67, while the free-standing tomb, where Torumtay was buried, was erected in 1278.

The entrance to the mosque is in its unusual north façade, which has a porch in the form of an *eyvan*, or vaulted alcove. High on either side of the porch there is a single arched window with stalactite ornamentation, and at the corners of the building there are cylindrical buttress towers on square bases. The attached *türbe* is on the left, set back from the façade of the mosque and joined to its side; this is square in plan and is covered by a sixteen-faceted dome carried by an octagonal drum revetted with turquoise tiles, most of which have disappeared. The prayer hall of the mosque is divided by two rows of four cruciform piers into three aisles, each of which has five domed chambers. The second chamber in from the entrance *eyvan* is covered with a star-shaped vault, at the center of which is a dome carried by a pyramidal roof.

The large free-standing *türbe* is square in plan, its southern façade pierced by a window framed in a large ogive arch, flanked with panels of palmettes in high relief and with ornamental pilasters at the corners. Each of these pilasters is one of three buttresses on either side, with the entrance on the south between the rectangular abutments there. The vaulted interior of the *türbe* contains the cenotaph of Torumtay and eight others, presumably members of

Gökmedrese Camii

Gökmedrese Camii, Drawing from Gabriel

his family, three of whom, judging from the small size of their caskets, died in early childhood.

A narrow lane leading left from the main avenue opposite Torumtay's *türbe* leads to an Ottoman mosque complex near the river. This *külliye* was built in 1428 by Yürgüçpaşa, a vezier of Mehmet I. The mosque is in the so-called Bursa style, which the Ottomans developed in their first capital, the Greek Prusias ad Olympium, during the century before their capture of Constantinople. An unusual feature of the mosque is that the chamber to the right of the entrance *eyvan* serves as the founder's *türbe*. Arrayed around the mosque courtyard are the other elements of the *külliye*, which include a *medrese* and a hospice.

We now continue toward the center of town along the narrow street just to the right of the main avenue. Some 200 meters along we pass on our right a ruined and unidentified Selçuk mosque, and then 100 meters beyond that we come to a pair of ruined tombs. The tomb on the right is the Şadgeldi Türbesi, dated by an inscription to 1381. The one on the left is the *türbe* of the Danışmendid emir Halifet Gazi, traditionally dated to 1145-46. Halifet Gazi is buried in a a splendid marble sarcophagus decorated with the heads of rams and gorgons decked with garlands, probably taken from a Roman tomb. In the little park between the tombs and the main avenue there are arrayed a number of ancient architectural remains, as well as fragments of beautifully carved inscriptions in classical Greek, but the structure to which they belonged has not been identified.

Two blocks farther along the main avenue we come to the Archaeological Museum. This is one of the most interesting local museums in Anatolia, with exhibits dating back to the early Bronze Age, ca. 3,500 B.C., from the Hittite, Urartian, Phrygian, Greek, Roman, Byzantine, and early Turkish periods, as well as an ethnographical collection with objects from the Selçuk and Ottoman eras.

The garden of the museum is used to display ancient architectural and sculptural fragments, as well as inscriptions and funerary stelae. The structure at the rear of the garden is the *türbe* of the Selçuk sultan Rüknettin Mesut I, who reigned in the years 1116-1156. The *türbe* itself was erected in the fourteenth century by the Ilkhanid Mongols. The *türbe* is used to display the mummified remains of six Ilkhanid nobles.

There are two more tombs on the side street that leads down to the river opposite the *türbe* of Sultan Mesut. The one on the right is the Şehzade Türbesi and that to the left the Şehzadeler Türbesi. The Şehzade Türbesi was built by Beyazit I in the last decade of the fourteenth century as the tomb of his son Osman, while the Şehzadeler Türbesi was erected in 1410 by Mehmet I to bury four Ottoman princes.

We continue down the street to the river road and turn right, and then after some 200 meters we come to the Beyazidiye, the imperial mosque complex of Beyazit II, the largest and most impressive Islamic monument in Amasya. The mosque was completed in 1486 by Beyazit's eldest son, Prince Ahmet, who was governor of Amasya. He was the heir apparent, but when Beyazit died in 1512 Ahmet's younger brother Selim I gained control of the Janissaries, the elite corps of the Ottoman army; and with their help he succeeded to the throne. A war of succession followed, ending the following year when Selim defeated and killed Ahmet.

The mosque stands in the middle of a large garden courtyard facing the river, its two minarets rising from the corners of the building behind the five-bayed porch, the one on the left fluted and the other decorated with a pattern of zigzags and palmettes. The mosque is preceded by a five-bay porch; in front of it there are two conical *şadırvan*s, or ablution fountains, the larger one in line with the mosque entrance and the smaller to the right.

The main area of the prayer hall is covered by two huge domes one behind the other, with the first one surrounded on three sides by smaller domes, separated from the inner area by the four piers that carry the northern dome. The side areas were used as dervish hospices, a feature found only in early Ottoman mosques and not in those of the classical period, roughly 1500-1800. The *külliye* also included a number of other institutions, of which there survive only

The Beyazidiye, Amasya

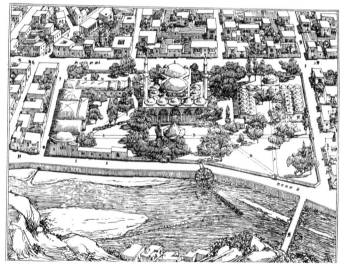

The Beyazidiye, Amasya, Drawing from Gabriel

the *medrese*, which is to the right of the mosque, as we face it from the river, and on the left the *imaret*, or free kitchen, which also served as a hospice. The *imaret* is still functioning, one of the very few Ottoman soup kitchens that continue to serve free food to the needy.

Leaving the Beyazidiye by the gateway on its western side, beyond the *medrese*, we turn right and walk down to the river, continuing to the other side on the third of the city's six bridges, counting from east to west. As we do so we see upstream near the left bank the last of the old water mills still functioning in Amasya. On the other side of the bridge we turn right and begin walking through the most picturesque part of town, a quarter of old stone and wooden houses that takes one back to Ottoman times.

About 100 meters along we come to a classical Ottoman mosque with its back to the river bank. This was founded in 1509 by Bülbül Hatun ("Lady Nightingale"), a wife of Beyazit II, who before he became sultan in 1481 had served as governor in Amasya. The mosque is preceded by a five-bay porch, with the single minaret rising behind it to the left at the corner of the building. The prayer hall comprises six square chambers, the two central ones domed and the two on either side covered by low cross vaults.

Just beyond the mosque a sign identifies the Hazaranlar Konağı, an Ottoman mansion on the riverside that has recently been restored and converted into an ethnographical museum and cultural center. The mansion was built in 1872 by Hasan Talat Efendi, who at the time was minister of finance in Istanbul. The rooms of the *konak* are furnished and decorated in their original style, evoking a memory of the graciousness of life here in late Ottoman times.

Another sign points the way to Kralkaya, or King's Rock, also known as Kızlar Sarayı, the Palace of the Maidens. This is a terrace, supported by a retaining wall, which was the site of the palace of the Pontic kings, of which not a trace remains. A pathway leads from the terrace to three of the dozen royal Pontic tombs that are carved out of the cliff face. These all date from the Hellenistic period, and one of them has been identified by an inscription as the

tomb of Pharnaces I (185-159 B.C.). The tomb at the end of the
pathway from the terrace, the one at the far left viewed from below,
was converted into a chapel in Byzantine times, and it still retains
some vivid frescoes that have been dated to the eleventh century.
Nearby is the entrance to one of the "tube-like channels" mentioned
by Strabo; these are tunnels that were cut through the acropolis
rock during the Hellenistic period, either as sally ports or passages
to springs. The tunnels are now blocked up and their lower entrances
are lost beneath the fallen rocks below.

We continue walking along the left bank as far as the next
bridge, the ancient Çağlayan Köprüsü, which is still supported by
the seven arches that were erected by the Danişmendid in the last
quarter of the eleventh century. We cross here and start walking up
the right bank of the river, which soon begins to make a huge S-
bend as it curves around the base of the great acropolis rock.

About 100 meters beyond Çağlayan Köprüsü we come to
Saraçhane Camii, the Mosque of the Saddlers' Han, built in 1399.
A highly unusual feature of the mosque is that its minaret rises
from the center of the side rather than from a corner of the building.
This is because the western half of the mosque is a late addition,
and the minaret was never moved from its original position to
compensate for this.

Another 150 meters along we come to the fifth bridge, Hükümet
Köprüsü, which on the right bank of the river leads to Hükümet
Meydanı, the main square of Amasya, centered on a large equestrian
statue of Atatürk. The square is dominated on its eastern side by
Gümüşlüzade Camii, a large mosque dating from 1326 but heavily
restored in modern times.

Some 250 meters beyond Hükümet Köprüsü we come to the
Yıldız Hatun Medresesi, better known as the Tımarhane, or Insane
Asylum. The *medrese* was built in 1308/09 for Sultan Olcaytu of
the Ilkhanid Mongols, who dedicated it to his wife Yıldız Hatun.
This was actually a *darüşşifa,* or hospital, with a section for mental
patients. Like other hospitals in Anatolia at the time it also served
as a medical school, with doctors continuing to be trained here until

Ottoman houses , Amasya

the nineteenth century. One of those who practiced medicine here was Serefettin ibni Ali, who in 1465 completed a work called *Kitab al-Jarrahiyya,* or the *Book of Surgery,* in which surgical operations were described and illustrated for medical students. The building is laid out on the plan of a typical Selçuk *medrese*, with an arcaded courtyard and two *eyvans*, and with arched windows flanking the monumental and ornately carved entryway, framed by towers at its corners.

A short way beyond the Tımarhane we come to Mehmet Paşa Camii, an Ottoman mosque built in 1486. The founder, Mehmet Paşa, served as regent for Şehzade Mehmet, son of Beyazit II, when the young prince was appointed provincial governor in Amasya. The plan of the mosque is unique. The prayer hall is a domed square with the minaret rising from its northwest corner; on either side tiny vaulted passages lead to two smaller square domed rooms, each of which is connected by passages to an identical room beyond. Fireplaces in the latter two rooms indicate that the side chambers were used to house travelling dervishes. Beyond the

The Tımarhane, Drawing by Gabriel

two western rooms there is a third chamber of identical plan, built as a *türbe* for Mehmet Paşa's father. Another unique feature of the mosque is its porch, which has six bays rather than the usual three or five, with the third bay from the left leading to the entryway of the prayer hall, thus putting the portico off-center with the building's façade. The beautifully carved *mimber* is one of the finest in Turkey.

After walking for another 400 meters we come to the last of the six bridges—Kuş Köprüsü—the Bridge of the Birds. About 100 meters upstream from the bridge, beyond an old *hamam* and hospice, we come to Beyazit Paşa Camii. This was completed in 1419 by Beyazit Paşa of Amasya, grand vezier under Mehmet I. This is another unusual building, with a five-bayed porch and an entrance *eyvan* flanked by side chambers, a prayer hall consisting of two domed squares in a row, and a pair of smaller domed squares on the side to house travelling dervishes. The porch is considered to be one of the most elegant in early Ottoman architecture.

We now retrace our steps and cross Kuş Köprüsü, after which we come on our right to Kapıağası Medresesi, still another unusual building. The *medrese* was founded in 1488 by Hüseyin Ağa, who served Beyazit II as Kapıağası, or Ağa of the Gate, a post held by the Chief White Eunuch. The building is octagonal in plan, with the entryway on the northeast, the *dershane*, or lecture hall on the south, and the student cells arrayed three in a row on each of the other six sides of the arcaded courtyard. The building still serves something like its original purpose, for it is now used as a Koran school.

Continuing along the road that leads in from the river past the *medrese*, we turn left on the road signposted "Kale." This leads uphill, and after about two kilometers takes us to the acropolis of ancient Amaseia. Originally the great stronghold of the Pontic kings, the citadel was subsequently occupied in turn by the Romans, Byzantines, Danişmendid, Selçuks, Ilkhanid Mongols, and Ottomans. Most of the present citadel walls are of Byzantine or Turkish construction, except for two towers of the Hellenistic period. The view from the citadel is superb, with all of Amasya in view along the winding river below.

Beyazit Paşa Camii, Drawing by Gabriel

Kapıağası Medresesi, Drawing by Gabriel

We now make our way back and cross Kuş Köprüsü, continuing straight ahead on the road that goes uphill to the Sofular quarter. Beyond the first intersection we pass on our left Şirvanlı Camii, built in 1892. Then, turning right at the next intersection, we come to Çilehan Camii, built in 1483 by the Chief White Eunuch Hüseyin Ağa. Above it, in a park, we find Pir İlyas Türbesi, dated 1487. Then about 300 meters to the west we come to Sofular Camii, founded in 1485 by Abdullah Paşa.

We now make our way back downhill and turn left on Atatürk Caddesi. This brings us back toward the center of town, and en route we will stop to look at some of the buildings on the hillside above.

The first of the monuments that we come to is Pazar Camii, built in 1483 by the Chief Black Eunuch Hüseyin Ağa, who that same year erected the nearby *bedesten,* or covered market. Walking westward for about 100 meters in the narrow winding streets to the left of the main avenue, we come to a group of three buildings: Kilerci Süleyman Ağa Camii, built in 1486; Taş Han, erected in 1758 by Hacı Mehmet Paşa; and Burmalı Minare Camii, the Mosque with the Spiral Minaret. The latter mosque was founded during the reign of Keyhüsrev II (1237-47) by two brothers who were members of his cabinet, the vizier Ferruh, and the treasurer, Yusuf, both of whom are buried in the octagonal *türbe* attached to the mosque.

About 150 meters north of Burmalı Minare Camii on the hillside we find Fethiye Camii, the Mosque of the Conquest. This was originally a Byzantine church that was converted into a mosque early in the Turkish period. An inscription records that the church was founded in 1116 by Helena, daughter of Caesar Phocas.

Before leaving Amasya we might drive out of town for three or four kilometers on the Tokat road to see the Ferhat Su Kanalı, an ancient watercourse hollowed out of the rock face of the mountain. Hamilton mentions this canal in his description of his approach to Amasya:

By degrees the rocky hills on each side approach so close, that the river two miles above Amasia flows through a narrow glen hemmed in between precipitous cliffs, where the road is cut along the mountain side, on the right bank of the river; about 20 feet farther up are the remains of an aqueduct, formed with considerable labour in the solid rock, or carried along the face of the cliff by artificial channels. It appeared to be the work of ancient times, and has long been useless.

Hamilton writes about the aqueduct again, at the conclusion of his description of Amasya, relating a local Turkish legend concerning the origin of the rock-cut watercourse.

I have already alluded to the aqueduct along the roadside on entering Amasia, and which Fontanier mistook for the watercourse mentioned by Strabo. The Turks of Amasia have a tradition respecting its origin, which is no bad specimen of their talents and ingenuity in this way. The story goes that there once dwelt in this neighbourhood a rich and powerful young man of the name of Fer-hat, who was in love with a beautiful damsel of Amasia. He offered her marriage, which she accepted on condition that he supplied her native town with water from a distant valley and performed all the work himself. Undismayed at the undertaking, he immediately set to work, and to judge from the result must have laboured hard for many a year. At length one day he met an old woman who, from true Turkish inquisitiveness, asked him what he was about; Fer-hat told her the story of his love, and that he hoped soon to have completed his task; whereupon she replied, that he might cease from his useless labour, as the maiden, who must by this time have passed her seventieth year, was dead. On hearing this he gave up his undertaking, and soon dying of a broken heart, was buried with the lady of his love on the summit of a neighbouring mountain.

After seeing the watercourse we make our way back to Amasya. We then retrace our route to Samsun, where we resume our drive eastward along the Black Sea coast.

CHAPTER FIVE

SAMSUN TO TRABZON: EXCURSIONS TO NİKSAR AND ŞEBİNKARAHİSAR

The next stage of our journey takes us from Samsun eastward across the delta of the Yeşilırmak, the ancient River Iris, which we cross at the village of Çarşamba, after a drive of 34 kilometers. Hamilton, who was travelling in the opposite direction, describes the countryside as it was in his day, before the Black Sea coast became part of the modern world:

On leaving Charshambah, the English-looking appearance of the country was much increased by the fine timber-trees growing in the hedges. At the third mile we crossed a stream, flowing I was told from a small lake on the west, called Turkman Bohar Ghieul. Farther on we passed through a grove of lofty elms, from the tops of which the branches of the wild vine hung down nearly to the ground; and as we advanced towards the hills on the left, we observed them stretching in a semicircular direction towards the sea, between us and Samsun; cultivation gradually ceased, the woods became more wild and tangled, and the ground wet and marshy. As we passed a small cafe soon after two, a number of peasants were drawn up in a line, and going through their devotions in the open air, under the direction of their Imaum or Hodja; their motions were performed simultaneously, with military precision, although when Turks perform their devotions in the open air, it is usual for them to do so singly.

Some 21 kilometers beyond Çarşamba we reach the eastern end of the delta at the little port town of Terme, which is at the mouth of the river known as the Terme Suyu. The names of the town and river are derived from their ancient ones: Terme having been identified as Themiscra and the Terme Suyu as the Thermodon.

Here again we refer to Hamilton for a description of the scene as it was in times past:

> The little town of Thermeh, which evidently derives its name from its proximity to the Thermodon, is on the left bank of the river, and consists of a few wooden houses, a wooden mosque, and a small bazaar. Vessels come up as far as the town for grain and rice, which they carry along the coast; these belong principally to the Pacha, who employs eight or ten of them in that trade. The cattle of Thermeh are handsome and larger than usual; and everything is produced in the greatest perfection in the province of Djanik, which extends from Unieh to Samsun, and from the sea-shore to the mountains to the S., which run in a vast semicircle from these two places, enclosing one of the richest plains in the world....From Thermeh to Charshambah the same character of country prevailed, but cultivation increased, and gardens increased. Flax and Indian corn were in abundance, and the oaks and elm-trees of larger size....Pheasants, deer, roebuck and wild boar are said to abound in the extensive forests which lie between the mouths of the Iris and the Melitsch Chai, beside the wild cattle, buffaloes and horses which I have mentioned.

Themiscra and the River Thermodon are described by Strabo in Book XII of his *Geography,* in the section immediately after his summary history of Amisus. He writes as follows:

> Themiscra is a plain; on one side it is washed by the sea and is about sixty stadia distant from the city [Amisus], and on the other side it lies at the foot of the mountainous country, which is well-wooded and coursed by streams that have their sources therein. So one river, called the Thermodon, being supplied by all these streams, flows out through the plain; and another river similar to this, which flows out of Phanaroea, as it is called, flows out through the same plain, and is called the Iris....Then the stream is received by Themiscra and by the Pontic Sea. On this account the plain in question is always moist and covered with grass and can support herds of cattle and horses alike

Marble Statue of an Amazon, Metropolitan Museum of Art, New York

and admits of the sowing of millet-seeds and sorghum-seeds in very great, or rather unlimited, quantities. Indeed, their plenty of water offsets any drought, so that no famine comes down on these people, never once; and the country along the mountain yields so much fruit, self-grown and wild, I mean grapes and pears and apples and nuts, that those who go out to the forest at any time in the year get an abundant supply—the fruits at one time still hanging on the trees and at another lying on the fallen leaves or beneath them, which are shed deep and in great quantities. And numerous also are the catches of all kinds of wild animals, because of the good yield of food.

Elsewhere, in Volume XI of his *Geography,* Strabo notes that this part of the Pontic coast was the traditional homeland of the fabled race of women warriors known as the amazons. Of them he says:

Themiscra and the plains above Thermodon and the mountains that lie above them are by all writers mentioned as having belonged to the Amazons... The Amazons spent ten months of the year off to themselves performing their individual tasks, such as ploughing, planting, pasturing cattle, or particularly in training horses, though the bravest engage in hunting on horseback and practice warlike exercises. The right breasts of all are seared when they are infants, so that they can easily use their right hands for any purpose, and especially that of throwing the javelin. They also use bows and arrows and light shields, and make the skins of wild animals serve as helmets, clothing and girdles. They have two months in spring when they go up into the neighbouring mountain which separates them from the Gagarians. The Gagarians, also in accordance with native custom, go thither to offer sacrifice with the Amazons and also to have intercourse with them for the sake of begetting children, doing this in secrecy and darkness, any Gagarian at random with any Amazon; and after making them pregnant they send them away; and the females that are born are retained by the Amazons, but the males are taken by the Gagarians to be brought up; and each Gagarian to whom a child is brought adopts the child as his own, regarding the child as his because of the uncertainty.

Apollonius mentions the Thermodon in Book II of *The Argonautica,* where he has the Argonauts land at the mouth of the river
on their voyage to Colchis in quest of the golden fleece:

> On the same day they rounded the distant headland that guards the
> harbour of the Amazons....And here in the bay beyond the cape, as the
> sea was getting rough, the Argonauts ran ashore at the mouth of the
> Thermodon....Had the Argonauts stayed here as they intended and
> come to grips with the Amazons, the fight would have been a bloody
> one. For the Amazons of the Doeantian plain are by no means gentle,
> well-conducted folk; they are brutal and aggressive, and their main
> concern in life was war, daughters of Ares as they were, and of the
> Nymph Harmonia, who lay with the god in the depths of the Acmonian
> wood and bore him girls who fell in love with fighting. But Zeus once
> more sent forth the North-West Wind, and with its help the Argonauts
> set out from the curving shore where the Amazons of Themiscra were
> arming for battle. I must explain that the Amazons did not all live in
> one city; there were three separate tribes settled in different parts of
> the country. The party on the beach, whose queen at the time was
> Hippolyte, were Themiscrans. The Lycastians lived apart, and so did
> the Chadesians, who were javelin-throwers.

Thirty kilometers beyond Terme, just before reaching Ünye, we
come to the seaside hamlet of Aynıkola. This is named for St.
Nicholas, patron saint of the local mariners, who dedicated a church
to him here on an islet connected to the mainland by a causeway.
The was already in ruins when Hamilton passed this way in 1836,
and it has since disappeared. He describes the countryside between
Ünye and Terme as follows:

> No remains of antiquity are now to be seen at Unieh, and I therefore
> started early for Charshambah, ten hours distant. After winding through
> the streets we crossed the promontory, on which the town is located,

and again descended to the shore, where, to the west of the point, the ruins of a Greek church were visible on a small rock in the sea....Leaving the seashore we crossed a rich flat country along smooth and grassy glades, surrounded by woods and shrubs, and dotted over with single trees, while other groves and plains equally verdant opened on each side, affording beautiful vistas and rides over a country uninterruptedly level for many miles. The trees near our road were not generally high, but were festooned with the long branches of the wild vine, the clematis, falling over from their topmost branches in the greatest profusion. To the south they assumed a very different character, being forest-trees of great size....Proceeding across the plain towards Thermeh, we saw many large herds of cattle, buffaloes, and horses, the property of Osman Pacha, the great proprietor of the district....

We now come to Ünye, a little port town on the site of ancient Oinaion. Nothing remains of the ancient city of Oinaion, but there are the ruins of a medieval fortress near the shore in the most sheltered part of the bay, perhaps built by the Byzantine emperor Andronicus I Comnenus (1183-85) before he ascended the throne.

The historic Castle of Oinaion, a famed Byzantine stronghold, has been identified as the ruined fortress known as Çaleoğlu, which is near the village of Kaleköy, some five kilometers south of Ünye on highway 560, the road to Niksar. The fortress takes its Turkish name from a local *derebey,* or "lord of the valley," who used it as his stronghold in the eighteenth century.

Andronicus I Comnenus held this castle as a sovereign fief for a brief period before he became emperor in Constantinople in 1183. Two years later he was deposed and assassinated, with his son and heir apparent David so brutally mutilated that he died shortly afterwards. David's two infant sons, Alexius and David, were spirited out of Constantinople and were given refuge by their aunt, Queen Thamar of Georgia. When Constantinople fell to the Latins in 1204, Alexius and David Comnenus and their Georgian supporters seized Trebizond and established an independent realm in the Pontus and in Paphlagonia. Thus began the empire of Trebizond, with Alexius and David Comnenus ruling it as co-emperors. These brothers founded a dynasty that was to last for more than two and a half centuries and an empire that would outlive the restored Byzantine Empire in Constantinople by eight years. David was known as the Grand Comnenus, a title that after his death in 1214 was passed on to his brother Alexius and subsequently to all of the other emperors of the Comneni dynasty in Trebizond.

After the Latins conquered Constantinople they drew up a document called the *Partitio Romaniae,* which listed the various fragments of the dismembered Byzantine Empire that would be divided up among the Venetians and the knights of the Fourth Crusade. The easternmost Byzantine possession listed in the *Partitio Romaniae* was Oinaion, but at the very moment that the list was being made Alexius and David Comnenus and their Georgian troops were taking control of the town and its castle, which thenceforth was part of the empire of Trebizond.

The fortress of Çaleoğlu has been identified as the legendary "Castle of the Sparrow Hawk, which apparently first appears in literature in the late fourteenth-century romance of *Melusine,* written by Jean d'Arrus. Melusine, whose name is also written as Melisande, was the supposed wife of Raymond, Count of Lusignan, who belonged to a dynasty that ruled both Cyprus and the Armenian kingdom of Cilicia. The princess Merlier, sister of Melusine, was, according to the romance, condemned to imprisonment in this castle until Judgment Day. She was guarded by a sparrowhawk, but chivalrous knights were assigned to stand vigil outside the castle. The knights were required to keep the sparrow-hawk awake and to remain outside the castle for three days and nights without sleep, sustenance, or company. As a reward, they were entitled to have the imprisoned princess grant them any wish, provided that they asked for "earthly things," but they could not "demand her body nor her love by marriage nor otherwise." Knights who made unsuitable requests suffered ill luck unto the ninth generation. After one such vigil a king of Armenia asked for the princess herself, and as punishment he and his descendants were beset by unceasing war.

The first to associate the legendary Castle of the Sparrow Hawk with this Pontic fortress seems to have been Johan Shiltberger, who joined the army of King Sigismund of Hungary in 1394 and who was captured by Beyazit I at Nicopolis in 1396 and then by Tamerlane at Ankara in 1402, after which he travelled through northeastern Asia Minor on his way to the Caucasus and Russia. In his account of his travels in the Pontic Alps he writes:

> There is on a mountain a castle, called that of the sparrow-hawk. Within it is a beautiful virgin, and a sparrow-hawk on a perch. Whoever goes there and does not sleep but watches for three days and three nights, whatever he asks of the virgin, that is chaste, that she will grant to him. And when he finishes the watch, he goes into the castle and comes to a fine palace, where he sees a sparrow-hawk standing on a perch; and when the sparrow-hawk sees the man, he screams, and the virgin comes out of her chamber, welcomes him and says: "Thou hast served me and watched for three days and three nights, and whatever thou now asks of me that is pure, that will I grant unto thee." And she does so. But if anybody asks for something that exhibits pride, impudence, or avarice, she curses him and his offspring, so that he can no longer obtain an honourable position.
>
> During the time that I and my companions were there, we asked a man to take us to the castle, and gave him money; and when we got to the place, one of my companions wanted to remain and keep watch. He who brought us advised him against it, and said that if he did not carry out the watch, he would be lost, and nobody would know where he went; the castle is also hidden by trees, so that nobody knows the way to it. It is also forbidden by the local Greek priests, and they say that the devil has to do with it, and not God.

Hamilton seems to have been the first foreign traveler to go in search of the Castle of Oinaion, which he was told of by his Greek landlord in Ünye:

> ...he said that the only object of interest near Unieh was a castle, built

on the summit of a lofty rock, about an hour off towards the interior, with wonderful flights of steps, treasures, baths, etc., excavated in the solid rock. I was anxious to see what had given rise to such a description, and accordingly at once put myself under the guidance of two Greek boys, and reached the foot of the castle-hill, after a walk of nearly an hour and a half up the valley of the Unieh Su....The castle is situated on the summit of a lofty and almost perpendicular rock, surrounded by deep glens and wooded hills, with here and there a grassy glade, above which it rises to a height of nearly 500 feet; to the south it joins the hills by a neck of land on which is a small Turkish village called Kaleh Kieui; yet even here the rock rises perpendicularly 200 feet, presenting to the view a tetrastyle temple cut in it halfway up the smooth face of the precipitous cliff, through which an opening leads into a small cave, where, according to tradition, a hermit formerly dwelt. It is now inaccessible; no ladder could ever reach it; and a narrow path scooped out of the face of the rock is almost obliterated. On each side of the temple are several paintings...apparently of Greek saints. The upper portion of the hill was so precipitous all round, that my guides in vain endeavoured to find a way to the top....

The temple noted by Hamilton is actually an ancient rock-hewn tomb of the temple type, its pediment decorated with the relief of an eagle with outstretched wings. The paintings that he describes would indicate that the tomb was converted to a Christian sanctuary during the Byzantine era.

Hamilton's visit to the Castle of Oinaion led him to the discovery of the local iron lodes, which he took to be those of the ancient people known as the Chalybes, described thus by Apollonius in Book II of *The Argonautica:*

At nightfall on the following day they reached the land of the Chalybes. These people do not use the ploughing ox. They not only grow no corn, but plant no vines or trees for their delicious fruit and graze no flocks in dewy pastures. Their task is to dig for iron in the stubborn ground and they live by selling the metal they produce. To them no morning ever brings a holiday. In a black atmosphere of soot and smoke they live a life of unremitting toil.

Hamilton first came upon evidence of these ancient iron lodes when he abandoned his first attempt to scale the precipitous heights to reach the Castle of Oinaion:

Full of disappointment for my want of success I descended to the valley, and prepared to return to Unieh; but on entering the woods I observed three or four black huts, which to my surprise I was told were iron-forges (Kaminosidero); my informant added also that the neighbouring hills were full of similar iron-works. It was a real pleasure thus unexpectedly to light upon the Chalybes, with their mines and forges, agreeing exactly with the words of the poet [Apollonius Rhodius]; there was, however, no one at work in them, and I could get no information as to how or when the ore was obtained....

Hamilton then goes on to write of his search for the source of the local iron and those who worked it:

Having produced horses and a guide I started for the mountains five miles off to the S. S. E., where I was to be conducted to an iron-mine. After ascending a narrow winding valley through the limestone rocks we reached the summit of the hills, where I observed many black tents of the Turcomans, or Kurds, of whom my Surici [guide] told me there were many in this neighbourhood. Proceeding in the same direction, the guide was soon at fault, and committed himself to the direction of a woman whom he met; she led us by a winding road, through thick natural woods and tangled coppices, to a sequestered spot, where we suddenly found ourselves in the presence of two men who were concealed amongst the bushes, and who, after a considerable parley, which I did not understand, got up and led the way. I thought myself in for an adventure; they would have had no difficulty in making me their prey, had they been so disposed; however I followed, and they soon brought me to a rude forge and hut, constructed of branches and trees. Here they spread a carpet and invited me to be seated, and to partake of their humble fare. I had brought no interpreter with me, and it was some time before they could be made to understand that I wished to see the mines from which the iron-ore was extracted. To this they replied that there were no mines, but that the ore was found everywhere about the hills near the surface. This they proved by scraping up the soil near their hut with a mattock, and collecting small nodular masses, which I understood was the form in which it was universally found in this district. The soil is dark yellow clay overlying the limestone rock to a thickness of two or three feet, and probably more in the hollows. The ore is poor, and the miners, like the Chalybes of old, must lead a hard and laborious life; they are at the same time charcoal-burners, for their own use; removing their huts and forges to a more productive spot as soon as they have exhausted the ore and consumed the wood in their immediate vicinity.

After seeing the Castle of Oinaion we might make a longer excursion south on highway 850 to visit Niksar, a drive of 105 kilometers.

Niksar is the Turkish form of Neocaesarea, the name that in the imperial Roman era was given to the ancient Pontic city of Cabeira. Cabeira was a temple city, which before the rise of the Pontic kings was ruled by priests of the Anatolian god Men, the male counterpart of the fertility goddess Ma. Cabeira became one of the principal strongholds of the Pontic kings, and Mithridates VI Eupator had a palace and hunting park here. Some of the most important battles in the turbulent career of Mithridates were fought in this part of the Pontus; and he was several times besieged in the fortress of Cabeira, whose impressive ruins still dominate the acropolis hill above the town. Neocaesarea and its fortress were captured from the Byzantines in 1073 by Gümüştekin Melik Ahmet Gazi Danişmend, founder of the Danişmendid dynasty, after which the town was called Niksar. Ahmet Gazi routed the knights of the First Crusade in 1100 in a battle near Malatya, where he captured Count Bohemund of Taranto and his cousin Richard of Salerno. Ahmet Gazi imprisoned

Bohemund and Richard for three years in the fortress at Niksar. The Selçuks destroyed a Crusader force sent to free the two captives, who were finally released in 1103 after the payment of a huge ransom. Otherwise Niksar had much the same history as the other cities of the region during the early Turkish period, except that its strategic position here at one of the gateways of the Pontus caused it to be fought over by all of the numerous forces that passed this way before the Ottomans secured final control over Anatolia.

Hamilton visited Niksar on 5 August 1836, en route to Amasya. As he only makes a passing mention of Niksar's Islamic monuments, we note that here, as elsewhere, Hamilton's interest centers on ancient Greek and Roman remains. Of Niksar Hamilton has this to say:

As we entered the town I saw several remains of ruined mosques and other edifices in the elaborate style of Persian or Saracenic architecture; and a broken sarcophagus near a fountain bore some evidence of an inscription which I was unable to decipher. From the road on the north side of town we overlooked the flat-roofed houses and gardens situated at the mouth of the valley; the castle, which is of considerable extent, stands on the brow of the hill to the north: it is a long and straggling mass, built at different periods, but in its present form is chiefly Turkish. In the gateways of the outer and inner walls were many large blocks of stone which had evidently belonged to older buildings, on two of which I found unimportant inscriptions....Amongst the walls near the summit of the castle were the remains of a handsome façade, containing three arches of good workmanship, apparently Roman, and belonging to an ancient edifice, on the ruins of which the modern fortress has been built. At a neighbouring fountain was a bas-relief representing a contest of animals, or rather two lions devouring a goat; and let into the wall close by were four stones with very rude sculptures, two of which represented animals and two men, one of whom was apparently a blacksmith. The castle was supplied with water by an aqueduct, part of which is still in use, the ruined portions being replaced by wooden pipes.

Niksar has a number of monuments from the early Turkish period, most notably its hilltop fortress, built by the Danişmendid on Byzantine, and possibly even Hellenistic, foundations. Beside the road leading up to the fortress we see the *türbe* of the Danişmendid emir Melik Ahmet Gazi, who died of an arrow wound in 1104 while fighting against the Byzantines. Within the citadel we find the ruins of Yağıbasan Medresesi, another Danişmendid monument, dated 1158. The oldest Danişmendid monument in the lower town is Ulu Cami; there is no dedicatory inscription, but tradition dates its founding to 1145. The only monument of the Ilkhanid Mongol period is Çöreğibüyük Camii, which has no dedicatory inscription, but it probably dates from the early fourteenth century; an interesting detail is the figure in relief of a sitting deer over the entrance portal.

We now retrace our route to Ünye, after which we resume our drive eastward along the Black Sea coast.

Some 24 kilometers beyond Ünye we pass Fatsa, the ancient Phadisana. A road leading inland is signposted for "Kale" (Castle). The castle is on a precipitous hilltop site five kilometers south of Fatsa, about 500 meters south of the village of Evkaf. Traces of four enceintes of walls survive, the inner one being the citadel. The area enclosed is oblong in shape, measuring 200 by 50 meters; the single gate, which is well preserved, is in the east side of the second enceinte from the outside. The castle, which is dated to the latter Byzantine period, was probably a stronghold of the empire of Trabizond.

Nine kilometers farther along the road we come to Bolaman, ancient Polemonion. Phadisana and Polemonion were two of the three coastal possessions of the inland city of Sidene, the third being Chabaca. Polemonion, which was originally known as Side, was renamed after himself by Polemon II, the last king of Pontus, who abdicated to the Romans in A.D. 64. Strabo mentions Sidene and its strongholds in his description of the Pontic coast, referring to Phadisana as Phabda.

After Themiscra one comes to Sidene, where there is a fertile plain, although it is not well-watered like Themiscra. It has strongholds on the seaboard: Side, after which Sidene was named, and Chabaca and Phabda. Now the territory of Amisus extends to this point, and the city has produced men noteworthy for their learning, Demetrius, the son of Rhatenus, and Dionysodorus, the mathematicians,...and Tyrranion, the grammarian, of whom I was a pupil.

Hamilton here again describes the lush vegetation we still see along this coast despite unsightly modern building development:

I left Fatsah at ten A.M. for Unieh, distant six hours; and after passing the fort, forded the Electchi Su. The wooded hills on the left were covered with medlar, pear, apple, and plum trees, all growing wild, and mingled with the bays, azaleas, and rhododendrons. After fording another river in a low and wooded plain, we again reached the shore, where I picked up some beautiful pebbles of jasper and agate.

As soon as we reach Bolaman we see a most remarkable building on the shore, a huge old wooden *konak* perched atop the substantial remains of a medieval castle. The castle, known as Bolaman Kalesi, is built on a rocky promontory that projects into the sea, with the remains of an outer perimeter wall still evident. The walls of the castle are made of large, roughly shaped stones whose mortar has been mostly washed away by the sea. The polygonal apse of a Byzantine chapel projects through the east wall of the castle. The house that surmounts the castle was built in the first decade of the nineteenth century by Süleymanzade Hazinedaroğlu of Çarşamba, who was made paşa of Trabzon in 1811. He had a palace in Ünye and used the *konak* in Bolaman to house his family. The chapel is dated to the thirteenth or fourteenth century, while the castle probably dates from earlier in the Byzantine era.

Nearby there are also the ruins of an octagonal Byzantine church dedicated to St. Constantine the Great, dated between the seventh century and the tenth. There are also the remains of a thirteenth-century church dedicated to St. Barbara.

The great cape that forms the eastern end of the bay on which Fatsa and Bolaman are located is Yason Burnu, or Point Jason, known in antiquity as Iasonion Akrotirion. This is the largest promontory on the Turkish coast east of Sinop, projecting 14 kilometers into the sea in three points: Yason Burnu on the west, Çam Burnu on the east, and in between Çapraz Burnu. Çam Burnu, or Pine Cape, was known in antiquity as Genetes Akrotirion, after a local people known as the Genetes, who apparently built a temple on this headland dedicated to Genetaean Zeus. Apollonius mentions this cape in Book II of *The Argonautica,* describing some of the strange folk ways of the primitive people who dwelt in the mountainous hinterland beyond the promontory:

> ...the Argonauts rounded the headland of Genetaean Zeus and sailed in safety past the country of the Tibareni. Here, when a woman is in childbirth, it is the husband who takes to the bed. He lies there groaning with his head wrapped up and his wife feeds him with loving care. She even prepares the bath for the event.

Bolaman Kalesi

Next day they passed the Sacred Mountain and the highlands where the Mosynoeci live in their mosynes or wooden houses from which they take their name. These people have their own ideas as to what is right and proper. What we as a rule do openly in town or market place they do at home; and what we do in the privacy of our houses they do out of doors in the open street, and nobody thinks the worse of them. Even the sexual act puts no one to the blush in this community. On the contrary, like swine in the fields, they lie on the ground in promiscuous intercourse and are not at all disconcerted by the presence of others. Then again, their king sits in the loftiest hut to dispense justice to his numerous subjects. But if the poor man happens to make a mistake in his findings, they lock him up and give him nothing to eat for the rest of the day.

Apollonius based his description of the Mosynoeci on Xenophon's account of these peculiar people in his *Anabasis*. Xenophon had this to say about them:

Some boys belonging to the wealthier class of people [of the Mosynoeci] had been especially fattened up by being fed on boiled chestnuts. Their flesh was soft and very pale, and they were practically as wide as they were tall. Front and back were coloured brightly all over, tattooed with designs of flowers. They wanted to have sexual intercourse in public with the mistresses whom the Greeks brought with them, this being the normal thing in their country.

Strabo, too, writes of the Mosynoeci, whom he also calls the Heptacometae and the Byzeres, describing them thus in Book XII of his *Geography:*

Now all these people who live in the mountains are utterly savage, but the Heptacometae are worst than the rest. Some also live in trees or turrets; and it was on this account that the ancients called them "Mosynoeci," the turrets being called "mosyni." They live on the flesh of wild animals and on nuts; and they also attack wayfarers, leaping down upon them from their scaffolds. The Heptacometae cut down three maniples [six hundred men] of Pompey's army when they were passing through the mountainous country; for they mixed bowls of the crazing honey which is yielded by the tree-twigs, and placed them in the roads, and then, when the soldiers drank the mixture and lost their senses, they attacked them and easily disposed of them. Some of these barbarians are also called Byzeres.

The road passes through a long tunnel as it goes out around the peninsula. After it emerges we see on our left the lighthouse on Çam Burnu; then we have a view ahead of the bay at Perşembe, a fishing village known to the Genoese as Porta Voon. Then, after passing the ruined medieval fortress at Bozukkale, we come to Ordu.

Ordu stands on or near the site of ancient Cotyora, founded by colonists from Sinope in the eighth century B.C. Cotyora was one of the places where the Ten Thousand stopped on their homeward journey along the shore of the Euxine, as Xenophon writes in his *Anabasis*.

> ...they arrived at Cotyora, a Greek city and a colony of the Sinopeans, situated in the territory of the Tibarenians. There they remained forty-five days. During this time they first of all sacrificed to the gods, and all the several groups of the Greeks, nation by nation, instituted festal processions and athletic contests.

Xenophon was so favorably impressed by Cotyora that he seriously considered founding a new city in its vicinity, but the opposition of the Sinopeans persuaded him otherwise. Thus in the end he decided to continue on with the Ten Thousand, who set sail from Cotyora to Heracleia Pontica.

Cotyora does not seem to have survived the classical era, for there are no references to it in medieval sources, and Ordu appears to be a relatively modern foundation. The only places of interest in the town are the Paşaoğlu Konağı, an Ottoman mansion that has been restored as a museum, and the former Greek Orthodox cathedral, a domed basilica dating from 1856. The town was inhabited principally by Greeks and Armenians in Hamilton's time, with the Turks mostly living in scattered little communities or isolated huts around it. Of it Hamilton writes:

> The town contains 120 Greek and Armenian houses; the Turks, as in many places along the coast, where they are the principal if not the sole proprietors of the soil, live in single houses or small hamlets on the hills. In fact the manners of these Turks closely resemble those of their predecessors in the time of Xenophon, who describes them as dwelling in detached and insulated huts throughout the country. He also calls them barbarous and quarrelsome; and it is only within a few years that the feuds and disputes of neighbouring districts have been put down by the energetic interference of the government.

Some 46 kilometers beyond Ordu we come to Giresun, the ancient Cerasous. The seagirt site of the ancient city, now surrounded on its landward side by the modern town, is described by Bryer and Winfield as follows:

> Between Sinope and Trebizond the ruins of this city are the most significant along the coast and its now deserted acropolis rock bears witness to its importance in former times. The salient feature of this site is the great rocky peninsula which juts out into the sea and provides with Sinope, the best defensive site along the coast.

Cerasous was founded by colonists from Sinope in the eighth century B.C. Pharnaces I took Cerasous soon after capturing Sinope in 183 B.C., whereupon he renamed it Pharnaceia. Pharnaceia was captured by Lucullus in 71 B.C. and by Pompey in 64 B.C., but it was not annexed by Rome unil A.D. 64; in the interim it was held by the Galatian chieftain Deiotarus; by Darius III, grandson of Mithridates VI Eupator; and by Queen Pythodoris, widow of Polemon I. Tradition has it that it was from here that Lucullus

Giresun, View from Fortress Eastward

Giresun, Church of St. Nicholas

brought back the cherry tree to Italy, a legend that probably stems from the fact that the Latin word for cherry *is cerasus*. There appears, however, to be no basis for this charming story. The classical name for the city was revived in the Byzantine era and was used by the local Greeks up until 1923, when they were deported from Turkey in the population exchange that followed the Graeco-Turkish war of 1919-22. Alexius II Comnenus won a crucial victory over the Turks here in 1301, which enabled the Grand Comneni to retain the surrounding area up until the time that Trebizond finally fell to the Turks in 1461.

The site of ancient and medieval Cerasous was on the acropolis hill that forms the western side of Giresun's harbor, a volcanic spur that juts about a thousand meters into the sea, joined to the mainland by a low isthmus on the south. The impressive remains of the city's walls and its citadel can still be seen on the acropolis, along with the remains of two gates, of which the higher one on the southeast led to the inner fortress and the lower one on the southwest to the walled town. Hamilton thoroughly explored these walls, which he describes as follows:

> The town of Kerasunt, which represents the Pharnacia of antiquity...is situated on the extremity of a rocky promontory connected with the main by a low wooded isthmus of a pleasing and picturesque appearance. The highest point is crowned with the ruins of a Byzantine fortress, from which a strong wall, with Hellenic foundations, stretches down to the sea on both sides....
>
> Under the guidance of a chavasse [*çavus,* or sergeant], I examined the Hellenic walls, which are constructed in the best isodomous style. Commencing near the beach on the west, they continue in an easterly direction over the hill, forming the limits of the present town. Near the gateway they are upwards of 20 feet high, and form the foundations of the Agha's *konak*; a small mosque has also been raised upon the ruins of a square tower; the blocks of stone, a dark green volcanic breccia, are of gigantic size. Near the crest of the hill, where the wall runs N. N. E. for some distance, are the ruins of a more modern castle, attributed

Giresun, 1701, Print from Tournefort

Giresun, 1846, Drawing by Laurens

to the Genoese or Byzantines, and called the Utch Kaleh [Inner Castle] and on one of the angles of the wall is a small wooden fort with loopholes for musketry, said to have been erected by a powerful Dere Bey, who held possession of the place. To the east also the ancient walls may be traced almost the whole way from the castle to the sea, where I observed an arched Hellenic gate blocked up with masonry of the same style...beyond which was a high tower overgrown with ivy.

Having reached the shore, I returned by the beach, where the walls are entirely Byzantine, and where are the ruins of a small Byzantine church, built of well-hewn square stones, cemented together with mortar, with considerable remains of painting on the inside. These walls were very perfect on the west side, and passing through them by a postern gate I descended to the ruins of another church near the beach, where is a small harbour, fit only for very small vessels. Here was a double line of walls, the defences having been made double on this side, partly to defend the neighbouring port, and partly because, from the depth of the water, it was the only spot where an enemy's vessels could approach the shore in safety....

The former Greek Orthodox church of St. Nicholas in the lower town has been restored and is now open as a museum. The Greek sea captains of the town in times past left offerings here in the form of models of their ships, in thanksgiving to St. Nicholas, their patron saint. One of these was Captain Yorgakis Constantinos, who after retiring from the sea was made a paşa by Sultan Abdülhamit II (r. 1876-1909). The church of St. Nicholas was probably the source of the "Cerasous Gospels," an illuminated work of the eleventh century found in Giresun in 1906.

The great rock that rises above the shore on the eastern side of Giresun harbor is known as Gedik Kaya. The rock is surmounted by the ruins of a Byzantine fortress, erected to protect the city from being attacked by invaders crossing the Pontic mountains on the road that comes from Şebinkarahisar. The Gedik Kaya fortress was built or reconstructed by Alexius III Comnenus of Trebizond after 1362.

At this point we will make an excursion south across the mountains to Şebinkarahisar on highway 865, a drive of 93 kilometers that crosses the Eğribel Pass at an altitude of 2,200 meters.

Şebinkarahisar has been identified as the ancient Koloneia, whose ruined fortress still surmounts the great craggy rock that towers above the town, described thus by Bryer and Winfield:

> The great basalt rock of Koloneia rises abruptly out of a rich plain, the
> floor of which is about 1450 m above sea-level, and is surrounded on
> three sides by arid alum-streaked mountains, and by an exit to the
> Lykos valley to the south. The rock is-about 1000 m long, 500 m wide
> and 160 m high. It stands nearly sheer "like an Ark alone in the midst
> of a sea of flowers," except for a steep slope to the south-west. this
> gives access from the town, or *vicus,* up to the principal, and what
> appears to be the only, entrance to the castle.

Procopius, in his *Wars,* writes that it was Pompey who called the city Koloneia, which leads one to suppose that he settled a colony of Roman veterans here after the conclusion of the Mithridatic Wars in 63 B.C. But there was almost certainly a city already in existence here, as evidenced by prehistoric habitation mounds and by the great strategic importance of the site. Procopius also writes that Justinian (r. 527-65) made considerable efforts to strengthen the defences of Koloneia, which was probably first fortified by the early Pontic kings. The fortress was known as Mavrokastron, the Black Castle, which in Turkish became Karahisar. Still later it was called Şebinkarahisar, from the alum (*şebin*) which was its principal export. The city was taken by the Turks soon after the battle of Manzikert, falling to the Saltukid emirs of Erzurum. It was then taken in turn by four Türkmen emirates, the Mengüçekid, Eretnid, Akkoyunlu (White Sheep), and Karakoyunlu (Black Sheep). Then after Mehmet II defeated the Karakoyunlu under Uzun Hasan in 1471, Şebinkarahisar became a permanent part of the Ottoman Empire. The town was devastated by a terrible earthquake in 1939, which destroyed all of its Islamic monuments. One of these, Fatih

Camii, built by Mehmet II soon after his victory over Uzun Hasan, has since been restored, though in a style different from the original. The great fortress above the town was also severely damaged in the earthquake, but it is still a most impressive sight, its walls completely surrounding the summit of the great basalt rock.

There is a ruined monastery seven kilometers due east of Şebinkarahisar, at the place known as Kayadibi. The monastery, which was dedicated to the Panayia Theotokos, the Virgin Mother of God, is built around a cave high up in the face of a precipitous cliff. Tradition has it that the monastery was founded by St. John Isocastis, who was bishop of Koloneia in the years 481-90. Most of the surviving monastic structures, however, are thought to date from the nineteenth century.

We now retrace our route to Giresun, after which we resume our drive eastward along the coast.

Some four kilometers beyond Giresun we see the offshore islet known as Giresun Adası. This was known in antiquity as Aretias,

Islet between Giresun and Tirebolu

the Isle of Ares, the god of war; and it, according to legend, had been a shrine of the amazons. The Argonauts had been warned of this by King Phineus when he gave them directions for their journey, as we read in Book II of *The Argonautica:*

Opposite Helice the Bear there is a foreland called Carambis, steep on every side and presenting to the sea a lofty pinnacle which splits the wind-stream from the North in two. When you have rounded this, the whole length of Aegialus will lie before you. But at the very end of it the coast juts out, and there the waters of Halys come down with a terrific roar. Near by, the smaller River Iris rolls foaming to the sea, and farther east a great and lofty cape is thrust out from the land. Then comes the mouth of the River Thermodon, which, after wandering across the continent, flows into a quiet bay by the cape of Themiscra. Here is the plain of Doeas, and the three towns of the Amazons near by. The Chalybes come next, a miserable tribe, whose land is rugged and intractable; but they toil away and work the iron that it yields. Near them live the sheep-farming Tibareni, beyond the Genetaean Cape, sacred to Zeus, the strangers' god. Next, and marching with them are the Mosynoeci. These people occupy the forest lands below the mountains. They built their wooden houses in the form of towers, which they call "mosynes," taking their own name from their well-constructed homes. When you have left these behind, you must beach your ship on a low-lying island, though not before you find some means of driving off the innumerable birds that haunt the lonely shore and pay no deference to man. Here the Queens of the Amazons, Otrere and Antiope, built a marble shrine for Ares when they were going to war. And here I advise you—and you know I am your friend —to stay a little while; for a godsend will come to you out of the bitter brine. But I must not sin again by telling you in detail all that I myself foresee.

Later Apollonius later writes of what happens when the Argonauts land on Aretias, how they were attacked by the war-god's vicious birds, who bombarded them with pointed feathers like winged darts, wounding "the noble Oileus." The Argonauts finally frightened away the birds by shouting, waving their crested helmets, and banging upon their shields with their swords and spears, after which they landed the *Argo* on the islet. There they were surprised to meet the four sons of Phrixus, who died in Colchis. The young men explained to Jason that they had been shipwrecked upon the islet on their voyage from Colchis to Boeotia, where they had hoped to recover the estate of their late grandfather, King Athamas of Orchomenus. Jason explained that he was a kinsman of theirs on their father's side, and he assured them that he would help them to resume their journey. Apollonius continues the story as follows:

> With that he [Jason] gave them clothing from the ship, and then the whole party made their way to the temple of Ares to sacrifice some sheep, and quickly took their places round the altar. It was made of small stones and stood inside the temple, which had no roof. But inside a black rock was fixed on the ground. This was sacred, and all the Amazons used at times to pray to it. But it was not their custom, when they came over from the mainland, to make burnt offerings of sheep or oxen on this altar. Instead they used the flesh of horses. They keep great herds of them.

On the islet there are the ruins of a defense tower and a monastery, both from the Byzantine period. Nothing remains of the temple of Ares, but the black rock that the Amazons prayed to is still an object of local veneration, particularly on 20 May, the feast day of the mystical Muslim saint Hıdrellez. On that day the locals row out to the islet and form a circle around the rock by joining hands, after which each of them takes a pebble and inserts it into one of the fissures of the black rock, making a wish for the future year.

Continuing eastward, we soon cut inland across the base of another promontory named Çam Burnu, the ancient Zephyrion Akrotirion. As we do so we pass the ruins of an ancient seagirt fortress known as Kalecik. The fortress may date back to the early

Byzantine period, perhaps even to the Roman era.

Between here and the next seaside village, Espiye, a road leading inland is signposted for Andoz Kalesi, which is on a hilltop site a short way up the left bank of Yağlıdere. The fortress, which dates from the latter Byzantine period, may have been the acropolis of a local settlement, perhaps on the site of modern Espiye.

The picturesque port town of Tirebolu stands on the site of ancient Tripolis, from which the present Turkish name is derived. The Greek name means "the three cities," a common toponym in Greece, in this case meaning that the town stands on three sea-girt promontories, almost islands. The promontories to the east and west are fortified. The western fortress—Çürükkale—is Ottoman, while the eastern one—Kurucakale, also known as the Castro—is Byzantine, the site of the acropolis of the city in both ancient and medieval times. Kurucakale is one of the most impressive fortresses on the Turkish coast of the Black Sea, apparently a work of the Grand Comneni of Trebizond. The French traveler Cuinet in 1890 reported that in the fortress he saw sculptures, probably reliefs,

Tirebolu, Easternmost Fortress

representing the Grand Comnenus John II (1280-97) and his wife, the empress Eudocia, daughter of the Byzantine emperor, Michael VIII Palaeologus. John married Eudocia in 1282, the first dynastic wedding between the Palaeologues of Constantinople and the Comneni of Trebizond.

Hamilton explored Tirebolu in the company of a representative of the local Ağa, whose *konak* was on one of the three promontories, presumably Çürükkale. Of it he writes:

> ...I proceeded, in company with the Agha's saraff, or banker, to visit the old castle at the extremity of the rock on which the *konak* is situated; this rock forms one of three distinct headlands on which the town of Tripolis or Tireboli is placed, with three intervening bays or harbours, and from which the ancient town probably derived its name. In these bays there is very deep water; but as they also contain many sunken rocks, the anchorage is not safe. The castle itself was much ruined, with some rudely carved stones over the gateway; a small battery of four guns has lately been erected here for the defence of the town, but the embrasures are so placed that two of the guns can only be brought to bear upon the town itself. On the summit of the rock are the remains of a small Byzantine church. The ruins of another castle and walls of considerable age exist on one of the other headlands, but no remains of Hellenic times are anywhere to be seen. The population of Tripolis is said to occupy 400 Turkish and 100 Greek houses; the town contains a bath, four mosques, and a Greek church....

Five kilometers beyond Tirebolu the road crosses the Harşit Çayı, the Philabonitis of the Greeks, a turbulent river that rises far up in the Pontic mountains. The view of the river valley from the coast is wild and picturesque, with a succession of heavily forested mountain chains rising above one another tier upon tier far into the blue distance, their foothills covered with dense growths of mulberry and wild cherry trees, with occasional rice fields on little terraced clearings. This is one of the most beautiful stretches of the Black Sea coast of Turkey, the road winding between densely wooded

Tirebolu, 1701, Print from Tournefort

Tirebolu, Kurucakale, Drawing by Laurens

hills intersected by numerous ravines with torrents flowing down from the towering mountains, the blue sea glittering through the verdant screen of tall trees and dense shrubbery. A short way up the river the Castle of Petroma towers on a hillside to the south, its ruined walls rising from a crag that drops sheer some 400 meters into the torrential river below. On the shore farther along we see a second ruined fortress known as Karaburun Kalesi; like Petroma, this is yet another stronghold of the Byzantine period, when the whole of the Pontic coast fairly bristled with castles.

Here again Hamilton describes the scene, writing of his approach to Tirebolu, where he refers to Karaburun Kalesi as Goolak Kaleh and the Harşit Çayı as the Tirebolu Su:

> We started soon after twelve, crossing the Eleheu Dere Su flowing through the plain, and two miles farther the Kara Burun Chai - a large river issuing from a wooded valley. The course of all these rivers, from their sources to the sea, must necessarily, owing to the geographical structure of the country, be extremely short; I was therefore surprised at the considerable body of water that many of them contained. The hills were covered with natural woods of mulberry and cherry trees; and although the same beautiful scenery continued over several successive ridges and intervening plains, we experienced much delay and inconvenience from the difficulty of getting the baggage horses through several narrow passes....
>
> Soon after two we had a fine view of the bold headland of Kara Bouroun about a mile off, with high rocks rising through the trees, and verdure which clothed its sides down to the water's edge; and we presently passed a few isolated rocks near the beach, on one of which were some ruins called Goolak Kilisseh, or Goolak Kaleh. We then crossed in succession two considerable streams, called the Baba Dere Su and the Bazar Chai; between these are a few small rice fields, which being then flooded resembled stagnant ponds or marshes overgrown with weeds and grass. Beyond the Bazar Chai we entered another plain formed by the detritus brought down by the Tireboli Su, which flows through its western portion. This river, rising in the

mountains of Armenia above Gümischkhana, and receiving many tributaries from these lofty hills, was so deep and rapid that we could only cross it by means of a ferry-boat, which delayed us some time, as we had to wait for the ferryman, and it required four trips before all the horses could be carried over.

The view of the valley presented much wild and picturesque scenery; many rocky pinnacles rose from its wooded sides, and a succession of mountain-chains was visible one above the other far into the interior. After crossing the ferry we ascended the hills to the N. W., and at half-past four reached the summit of the ridge, consisting of stratified beds of coloured marls and sands; and thence crossed a succession of ridges, through scenery of great beauty, amidst which the town of Tireboli embosomed in wooded hills overhanging the sea was conspicuous....

Twenty kilometers beyond Tirebolu we come to Görele, the ancient Philocaleia. Here a road leads inland to Kuşköy, or Bird Village, a drive of 28 kilometers Kuşköy is aptly named, since the villagers are renowned for their ability to communicate across intervening valleys with their shrill "whistle talk," which is believed to be an ancient language indigenous to remote regions such as the Pontic Mountains, or so say articles in prestigious publications such as the *New York Times.*

Fifteen kilometers beyond Görele we pass the village of Eynesil, and a short way beyond that we go by the promontory known as Görele Burnu, where there is a cluster of four ruined fortresses of the Byzantine period. This is the site of ancient Coralla, whose citadel was probably the ruined fortress known as Görele Kalesi. Coralla dates back to the classical era; but the ruins of the fortress probably date from the time of the Grand Comneni of Trebizond, who rebuilt the citadel and the city walls. Coralla continued to be a sizable Greek community after the fall of Trebizond to the Ottomans in 1461, and in the late sixteenth century it had 134 Christian households and only seven that were Muslim. Later it became the coastal stronghold of the rebellious Üçüncüoğlu clan, who ruled the Harşit valley from their mountain fortress at Torul. Then in 1811 the Ottoman government sent Süleyman Paşa of Trabzon to put down the rebels. He attacked Coralla from both land and sea, annihilating the Üçüncüoğlu and destroying the town, which thenceforth remained an uninhabited ruin.

Some 15 kilometers beyond Eynesil we come to Vakfıkebir, ancient Ethlabopiastes. A secondary road leads inland from here to the village of Tonya, a drive of 21 kilometers The people of this and the neighboring villages, the Tonyalı, are Greek-speaking Muslims; the men are feared throughout the Pontus because of their ferocity and violence, their two leading clans having killed one another off for generations past in an apparently endless vendetta. The Tonyalı and other Greek-speakers of the Pontus are probably descendants of the fierce Byzantine peasants who held these valleys in the time of the Grand Comneni, and who then afterwards converted to Islam, a common practice among Christians in Anatolia after the Turkish Conquest. The Greeks of this region, known in Byzantium as the Matzouka, were renowned warriors, and for centuries they protected Trebizond and the other coastal cities from the Muslim armies that tried to force their way through the Pontic valleys. They also fought against the intrusions of the Türkmen tribes and against the Laz, the Caucasian people who were their unwelcome neighbors around the eastern end of the Black Sea. Bryer and Winfield write thus of the redoubtable Greek mountaineers of the Matzouka:

Medieval Matzouka harboured the only sizeable number of Greek peasants in the interior of the Empire [of Trebizond], their farms meeting the grazing-lands of the Laz and Türkmen on three sides, which are annually disputed in May. Compared with the unreliable tributaries of the Grand Komnenoi on the southern and eastern fringes of their state, the Matzoukans were loyal to the central government (to which in the Middle Ages they contributed civil servants), formidable warriors, hardy traditionalists, pious benefactors, and patient farmers... The Matzoukans were noted for their belligerence, their resilience, and family cohesion. By fighting repeatedly for their lands along the Prytanis and Phyxitis they denied invaders access to Trebizond...then it was observed [by the Arab chronicler Al Umeri in 1300] that the defenders of the Grand Komnenoi, "although few in numbers and ill-equipped, are heroes, like implacable lions who never let their prey escape...." In 1361 they held the passes against the emir of Bayburt, slaughtering numerous infidels, whose heads they brought gleefully down to Trebizond.

The annual disputation of grazing lands between the Greek-speaking Pontic mountaineers, now pious Muslims, and their reasonably pacified Laz and Türkmen neighbors is perpetuated in the Kadırga festival, which is celebrated annually on May 20 at the common boundary point of the townships of Tonya, Torul, and Maçka, the latter toponym being a corruption of Matzouka. This is one of the many festivals which are held throughout the Pontus on that day and the two days following, to mark the annual return from the coast to the *yayla*s, the highland meadows so dear to the hearts of the Black Sea people. Sevan Nişanyan writes of this festival in his guide, *Zoom In—Black Sea:*

> Going up to the yayla is the most exciting event of the year. Many people who have left the land of their birth to live elsewhere come back each year merely for the sake of the yayla. Many regard the yayla as a cleansing experience, attributing to it an almost mystical aura....The yayla season formally begins on the first day of summer, which ancient tradition places on the "Sixth of May" (May 20 on the modern calendar)....Everywhere people feast and make merry in the fields....Then, for three days, they make music, dance the horon and soak themselves in alcohol.
>
> The horon is usually danced by men. Dancers stand in a circle holding hands. At first their steps are tentative, slow, even awkward. They gather speed as the music becomes wilder. The dance turns by degrees into the expression of an intense machismo, then increasingly into an explosive boiling frenzy. The name of the dance is a legacy of the Greek

choron and indicates a direct line of descent from the ancient Bacchic rites where celebrants went into a wild frenzy to honor the god of wine.

Merrymaking continues in the yayla in fits and starts... The veneer of city culture gets stripped off. Oxcarts replace taxis while people who normally wear suit and tie put on their traditional dress....Guests from other valleys arrive..., along with the traditional bards, professional wrestlers, trinket sellers and the best dancers of the province. For three days and nights they drink, dance, wrestle, fight and gamble. Eternal friends and mortal enemies are made. Handguns and bagpipes come out of winter storage. Cows and bulls are decked out in festive frills. At Hidirnebi, near Trabzon, participants form a thousand-person horon ring. At Kafkasör, above Artvin, they hold bull-fights. At Kadirga, at the intersection of the cantons of Maçka, Torul and Tonya, the three communities get together to re-enact long-forgotten hostilities. Everyone is welcome at the festivities. Every visitor becomes part of the ongoing show. And it is here in the breathtaking scenery of the mountains that the casual visitor first begins to penetrate the façade and catches a fleeting glimpse of the real spirit of the Black Sea.

Three kilometers beyond Vakfıkebir the road crosses Kirazlık Deresi, Cherry Valley. This valley perpetuates the name of the ancient Greek settlement known as Palaia (Old) Cerasous, which was so called to distinguish it from the later city of Cerasous farther west along the coast. Xenophon, in his *Anabasis,* notes that the Ten Thousand stopped here on the third day of their journey along the coast from Trebizond:

And on the third day of their journey they reached Cerasous, a Greek city on the sea, being a colony planted by the Sinopeans on the territory of Colchis. There they remained ten days; and the troops were reviewed under arms and numbered, and there proved to be eight thousand six hundred men. So many were left alive. The rest had perished at the hands of the enemy or in the snow, a few also by disease.

Beyond Kirazlık Deresi the road crosses the base of the huge promontory known as Yoros Burnu, the ancient Ieron Akrotirion, or Sacred Cape. A number of prominent capes in the Greek world bore this name, and often one finds the remains of a temple on the promontory, but here all that has survived is a ruined Byzantine fortress known as Yoros Kalesi.

As soon as we pass the cape we come to the village of Akçakale, the ancient Cordyle, where there is another ruined Byzantine fortress. Known variously as Akçakale or Cordyle Kalesi, this is one of the largest and best-preserved of the medieval fortresses on the Black Sea coast of Turkey, with its walls reaching a height of ten meters in places. Cordyle was the second port of Byzantine Trebizond and is mentioned frequently in chronicles of the empire of the Grand Comneni. The castle is celebrated in Pontic ballads, which tell of how the citadel was defended heroically by a Comneni princess who, after Trebizond fell to the Ottomans, threw herself from the battlements when all hope was lost rather than surrender to the Turks.

The coastal scenery along the eastern side of the cape is well described by Hamilton as he writes of his journey between Akçakale and Yoros Burnu:

> From Akjah Kaleh we descended to the shore, the coast here consisting of a succession of rocky headlands and intervening plains, protected by a reef of rocks which rises to the surface of the water about a mile from the shore. After passing Mersin, a single house upon the beach, with a boat drawn up before it, and crossing several small streams, we approached Cape Yoros, a mass of amygdaloidal trap; the scenery increased in wildness and grandeur at every step, as the road passed through thick woods of fruit trees, indigenous to the soil, as figs, cherries, mulberries, vines, chestnuts, pears, etc., while rhododendrons, azaleas, arbutus, and laurels, formed an impenetrable underwood, amidst which the fern grew most luxuriantly.

At the eastern end of the cape we come to Akçaabat, the Greek Platana. This town was the source of the "Platana Hoard," a collection of Byzantine coins now preserved in the Ashmolean Museum in Oxford. This treasure trove was buried in Platana at some time in the years 1285-92, as indicated by the coins of latest date in the collection. Two Byzantine churches have survived in Akçaabat, one of them dedicated to St. Michael and the other to the Incorporeal Saints. The latter church is dated by an inscription, which records that it was dedicated by the Grand Comnenus Manuel II to celebrate the victory that he won over a Turkish force on 30 August 1332, defeating a chieftain named Bayram Bey.

Hamilton writes of the church of St. Michael in describing Platana, the first town that he came to after leaving Trabzon. As he writes:

This town, which is said to contain 140 Greek and about 200 Turkish houses, is situated near the centre of an open bay which forms the winter anchorage of Trebizond, being less exposed to the N. W. gales than that of the roadstead. Having secured a *konak* in the cafe on the beach, I visited the old Greek church dedicated to St. Michael, and built, as the priest declared, about 800 years ago. Its style is certainly early Byzantine, and within are some curious old paintings on the screen before the altar, behind which four small columns rest on a low wall of the same material, and support a rude soffit. On the outside the windows and niches, several of which are false, are in rich Byzantine taste, decorated with several rows of an elegant beading or border. The priest was summoning his congregation to church on my arrival; and as the Greeks are not allowed the use of bells, they supply the want of them by a piece of wood suspended from a tree, which is struck like a drum by the priest, who at times endeavours to produce a kind of tune. The vine, the olive, and the fig grew here in great abundance, the vine being trained to the elms and mulberry trees planted in the hedges round every small enclosure; large quantities of tobacco are also raised.

Twelve kilometers beyond Akçaabat we enter Trabzon, the Greek Trebizond, the most important and historic city on the Black Sea coast of Turkey.

Hamilton describes the scenery along this shore as it was in times past, its beauty now considerably diminished by the strip developments that one encounters in the seaside suburbs of virtually all the coastal towns:

...For several miles to the west of Trebizond the ground rises gently from the sea, and is well cultivated, producing Indian corn and tobacco in abundance, as well as flax, melons, cucumbers, and beans.

Three miles from the town we crossed a small stream issuing from a wooded valley, and began ascending the low hills by a road overlooking the sea. The rocks, which here rise abruptly from the water's edge, consist of a decomposing trap conglomerate, and are covered with low woods and a great variety of flowers. Those which now chiefly scented the air were the yellow broom, gum-cistus, myrtle, arbutus, bay, heath, wild vine, and other creepers; but the rhododendrons were no longer in flower....At half-past two we descended to the gardens of Platana, where we saw the olive in great abundance....After proceeding along the beach for half a mile we reached the town of Platana, the greater part of which is situated up a delightful and well-cultivated valley, abounding in fruit and olive-trees.

CHAPTER SIX
TRABZON

Trapezous, known in times more recently past as Trebizond, was the third and easternmost of the three colonies that Sinope founded on the Pontic coast of Asia Minor in the eighth century B.C. Its traditional founding date, according to Eusebius of Caesarea, was 756 B.C., which would make it three years older than Rome and nearly a century older than Byzantium. The earliest mention of the city is in Xenophon's *Anabasis,* where he writes of the welcome that the Ten Thousand received here after finally crossing the Pontic Alps to reach the shores of the Euxine: "And the Trapezuntians supplied a market for the army, and received the Greeks kindly, and gave them oxen, barley meal, and wine as gifts of hospitality."

Trebizond seems to have enjoyed peace and freedom throughout the classical Greek and Hellenistic periods, and under the Romans it continued to have the privileges of a free city. The emperor Hadrian visited Trebizond in 129 and endowed the city with a new harbor, the remains of which were still visible in the mid-nineteenth century. The city was captured and badly damaged by the Goths in the years 263-70, and it lay in ruins until it was rebuilt during the time of Diocletian (r. 285-305). The defense walls were repaired and strengthened by Justinian, during whose reign Trebizond served as an advanced base for the Persian campaigns mounted by his great general Belisarius. During the time of Leo III (r. 714-41) Trebizond became capital of the Chaldean theme, the north-westernmost province of the Byzantine Empire. The strong fortifications of Trebizond, along with the great mountain barrier of the Pontic Alps and its valiant defenders, the Matzoukans, saved the city from being overrun by the Turks after the battle of Manzikert, with the heroic Theodore Gabras emerging as the effective ruler of the Trapezuntine region and defending it against a Georgian invasion.

The most illustrious era in the history of Trebizond began in

Trabzon, 1701, Print from Tournefort

1204, when Alexius Comnenus and his Georgian supporters took control of the city after the Latin conquest of Constantinople. At the same time David Comnenus conquered Paphlagonia and extended the boundaries of the new empire as far west as Heracleia Pontica. David, who ruled as co-emperor with his brother Alexius for ten years, was killed in battle against the Selçuks at Sinope in 1214, after which the western limits of the empire of Trebizond were pushed back to the River Iris. Alexius continued to reign until his death in 1222, to be followed by seventeen successive rulers of the Comneni line, including two women, a dynasty that lasted for 257 years.

The magnificence of Trebizond in the days of the Grand Comneni is the theme of an encomium by George Bessarion. Bessarion was born in Trebizond in 1399/1400 and went on to become Bishop of Nicaea and one of the leading figures in the late Byzantine renaissance. He left Constantinople before it fell to the Turks and settled in Italy, where he became a Cardinal in the Roman Catholic Church and twice almost became Pope. In Richard Stoneman's translation, Bessarion praised his birthplace in the following way:

> In such a land, in such a country, surrounded by mountains, hills, plains, and the sea of all seas the most gentle and friendly to men, our forefathers chose the most beautiful and secure spot to erect their city. It is a hill rising not very high above the land, cleft on either side with deep ravines and surrounded also as it were by ditches, far above the average of ditches. Through these, perpetual rivers run to the sea, fuller than usual in winter but not drying up in spring or even in summer, so that within there is not only perfect security but sufficient water for refreshment and for washing. Refuse and sewage can all be easily and lightly removed with their help, for the river runs so to speak before every front door. And this hill, which rises gently and unforested from the sea, climbs more steeply to the heights, is closed off on either side by ravines and hemmed in by cliffs, forming on top a high and level place suitable for dwellings and for the enjoyment of the different seasons. On this place, now an acropolis, they built, trusting in their own valour more in the site and their works; and yet they encircled it with strong walls, towers, battlements, and fortifications and so on, second to none.

Bessarion goes on to sing the praises of the famed "Golden Palace" of the Grand Comneni, which stood within the citadel on the highest level of the acropolis:

> The buildings of the palace are situated on the acropolis itself, and this acropolis is superior to any in the strength of its wall, the brilliance of its adornment, and the size and beauty of all of its features. The wall toward the west, which divides the acropolis and the public offices, serves the same purpose for both of them, rising to the second storey of the acropolis and the palace, and the wall above the public offices rises as much above that of the acropolis, as the latter does above the earth. The wall on either side, excellent in its workmanship, height and thickness...alone suffices to withstand any approaching enemy and to protect those inside; having a double gate and a single doorway,

it is built with entire security. On either side one area is set aside for the halls and the king's servants; in the centre is the palace, with its entrance raised up high and reached by a staircase. As you enter you are greeted by anterooms and vestibules, supreme in size and beauty, and wind vanes surround the building, facing in every direction to catch every breeze. On either side is a long building of great beauty, its foundation being all of white stone, and its roof decorated with gold and other colours, painted flowers and stars, emitting beams of light as if it were the heaven itself, remarkable for artistry and sumptuousness. All around the walls are painted the series of the kings, both of our own day and the days of our forefathers, and there are paintings of the dangers that our threatened city has overcome and of those who were worsted by our countrymen. Above it is the king's balcony with a pyramidal roof, supported by pillars in the form of monsters, and surrounded likewise by white stone lattices which reach up to the roof to keep the subjects from the kings. Here the kings appear to give instructions to the authorities, to speak with ambassadors, and to give audiences. Farther on is another royal balcony, much greater in breadth and height, roofed and colonnaded... where the king is wont to hold banquets for the authorities and the rest of his staff. Then on the left are a large number of rooms, one in particular with four walls and rectangular in shape, which contains images of the creation of the universe, of the origins of man and of his first societies. On the right are rooms and anterooms, wind-towers, bedrooms and chambers, divided by porticoes... all of indescribable beauty and decorated with fitting taste. And there is a holy church, brilliant with paintings and dedications of marvellous beauty.

The earliest extant description of the city by a western traveler is that of Ruy Gonzalez de Clavijo, who visited Trebizond in 1404 while en route to the court of Tamerlane as ambassador of Henry III of Castile. Clavijo has this to say about the city of the Grand Comneni:

The city of Trebizond lies beside the sea, and its encircling wall climbs over the hill slopes at the back of town. Here there is built a strong castle on a height that is protected by its own wall. On one side of the city flows a small river whose waters pass down a deep gorge, and this gives Trebizond a very strong defence in that quarter. On the other quarter there is a level plain, but the city wall is very strong. All around lie the suburbs, with many fine orchards. And this is a fine sight to see, for in its shops all the goods brought to the city are on sale. Close to the sea stand two castles, one belongs to the Venetians and the other to the Genoese, each of whom built their fortress with the consent of the Emperor. Outside the city are to be seen many churches and monasteries.

What follows is a description by Clavijo of his audience with the Emperor, Manuel III, who received him and his party in the imperial palace:

...the Emperor called for us ambassadors, sending horses and bringing us to his palace. On our arrival we found him in a chamber that was off a gallery, where he received us very graciously; and after talking for a time we returned to our lodging....The Emperor is a man well-built, tall and of a stately presence; he and his son were dressed in imperial robes, wearing hats of a very high shape which have cordings of gold running up the sides, with a great plume at the top made of crane feathers; further these hats were trimmed with marten fur.

After the fall of Constantinople to the Turks in 1453, and of the remaining Byzantine dominions in Greece within the following three years, Trebizond was the last outpost of Hellenic civilization, until it finally fell to the Ottomans in 1461 under Sultan Mehmet II, known to his people as Fatih, or the Conqueror. The last emperor of Trebizond, David II Comnenus was allowed to leave with his family and move to Adrianople (Edirne), but two years later he and his sons were executed by Fatih, bringing to an end the last imperial dynasty of Byzantium.

Trabzon, as it was known to the Turks, continued to be an

important city under the Ottomans, ranking as a provincial capital. Selim I served as provincial governor in Trabzon before he succeeded his father Beyazit II in 1512, and his son and successor Süleyman the Magnificent was born here in 1494. Trabzon was an important port and commercial center throughout most of the Ottoman era; it was the terminus of the caravan trail that passed through Erzurum to connect the Black Sea coast with Persia. The town also derived much of its sustenance from the sea, particularly from *hamsi* (a kind of anchovy), which has since time immemorial been a staple of the Pontic diet. Evliya Çelebi, in his *Seyahatname,* writes in praise of the *hamsi* caught and sold at Trabzon in his time, in the mid-seventeenth century. After describing the other fish sold in the market there, he says:

But the most precious of all, which frequently causes bloody strifes and quarrels in the marketplace, is the *hamsi balığı* taken in the season of Hamsan (the fifty days when southerly winds blow); these fish were formerly thrown down on the shore at Trabzon by virtue of a talisman erected, it is said, by Alexander, before the gate of the town, representing a fish of this kind in brass on a column of stone; but on the birth-night of the Prophet, when all talismans lost their power, the same happened to this at Trabzon; thus the fish are no longer thrown on the shore, but the sea abounds with them during the said fifty days. At this season boats loaded with these fish arrive in the harbor, and the dealers in fish cry them in a peculiar manner, and at the same time sounding a kind of horn or trumpet; as soon as this sounding is heard, the whole town is in an uproar, and people who hear it, even when at prayer, instantly cease, and run like madmen after it. It is a shining white fish of a span's length [22.8 centimeters], and is an aphrodisiac of extraordinary potency; strengthening and easy of digestion, does not smell like fish, creates no fever in those who eat it, and also cures sore mouths. If the head of this fish...is burnt, serpents and other venomous reptiles are killed by the smoke. The people use it during forty days in all their dishes, to which it gives a peculiar flavor... But however this fish may be dressed and eaten, it is extremely useful to

TRABZON

ᴜᴇ ꜱᴛᴏmach and eyes, and is a dish of friendship and love.

Most of Trabzon's trade was lost in the late nineteenth century, after the completion of the railway from Ankara to Erzurum and the subsequent construction of highways from there to Iran. During World War I Trabzon was occupied by the Russians from 1916 to 1918. In 1919 the city became part of the short-lived Greek Republic of the Pontus. In 1923 Trabzon lost all of its considerable Greek population in the exchange of minorities. The scars of war have long since healed and Trabzon has revived considerably in recent years; this revival is a part of the general resurgence of the Black Sea coast of Turkey.

The most famous of the churches and monasteries surviving from Byzantine Trebizond is just above and to the right of the highway as one enters the town from the west, a mile outside the bounds of the medieval city. This is the former church of Haghia Sophia, the Divine Wisdom, which was converted into a mosque in

Hagia Sophia, Trabzon, View from the Southeast

1511, according to Evliya Çelebi. The building was neglected and in poor repair when Hamilton saw it in 1836:

> The church of St. Sophia, close to the seashore, has been converted into a mosque by the Turks, and is in a sad state of decay. On the south side is an open porch in the Byzantine style, supported by two high slender columns, from which spring three round arches, contained within a larger one springing from each end; a small frieze, representing angels, saints, and other figures, much mutilated by the Turks, extends in a continuous line over the smaller arches. Above the center of the large arch is a carved figure of a double-headed eagle; a similar figure is let into the outer wall at the east end of the church, which is circular, as well as the two sides. The centre is octagonal, and built in a style very superior to the rest of the building. A neat border of echinus runs round it immediately below the roof, and another still more ornamental lower down. The walls within are stuccoed, and have been painted in fresco, but the Turks have almost entirely destroyed the paintings. The once-beautiful mosaic floor is also sadly injured; but in one of the compartments I found the representation of an eagle destroying a hare. The roof is supported by four handsome columns. Immediately adjoining is either a belfry or baptistery, in which there have been some fresco paintings, with Greek inscriptions stating whom they represented, and when and by whom they were executed, but so much injured that I could not make out the artist's name or the date of any of them.

The building remained derelict up until 1957, when a six-year program of restoration was begun by the Russell Trust Expedition, directed by David Talbot Rice. David Winfield was in charge of the work on the site. This program restored all of the surviving paintings in Haghia Sophia, as well as determining the architectural history of the church and its associated buildings. Haghia Sophia, the architectural masterpiece of the Byzantine empire of Trebizond, is now open as a museum.

Haghia Sophia was the conventual church of a now vanished

monastery, founded in the mid-thirteenth century by the Grand Comnenus Manuel I (r. 1238-63), who apparently commissioned the earliest of the paintings that were uncovered and cleaned in the restoration. The belfry was begun by Alexius IV (r. 1417-29) and completed by his son and successor John IV (r. 1429-58). John succeeded to the throne by murdering his father, whom he later commemorated in a painting together with himself on the exterior east face of the belfry, but this has since disappeared.

The church is set near the center of a large enclosure, with the belfry standing some 25 meters to the west. The modern entrance to the enclosure is on its southwest side, where we have a direct view of the south porch of the church, which is similar to the porches on its west and north sides, the eastern end terminating in a triple apse.

The basic plan of Haghia Sophia is approximately a cross in a square: four columns support the central dome on a high drum; the east bays of the aisles are barrel-vaulted and the long west bays cross-vaulted. At the eastern end of the church there are three apses; the central one is five-sided externally and those on either side are rounded. The southern side apse was part of a chamber that served as the diaconicon, or vestry, while the northern one was part of the prothesis, where the Communion was prepared. At the western end there is a narthex of the same width as the church, with a chapel above. Beyond this is the west porch, with similar porches on the north side. All three porches are great barrel-vaulted structures, each opening through a triple-arched arcade suported by a pair of marble columns.

The bay under the dome has a superb pavement in opus Alexandrinum, containing nine different kinds of marble. The four columns that support the dome are of Proconessian marble; they and their magnificent capitals may be from the church of St. Polyeuctes in Constantinople, completed in 525 and destroyed in the twelfth century. The capitals and columns of the porches are all reused marbles and are of various dates from the fifth century onwards. The south porch is one of the most remarkable features of

Hagia Sophia, Trabzon, Reliefs on South Porch

Hagia Sophia, Frescoes in Narthex

the church, principally because of its superb sculptured frieze. The figures in relief that make up the frieze are all on separate stones and represent the story of *Genesis,* with a single-headed eagle—the imperial emblem of the Comneni dynasty—on the keystone of the arch.

The paintings that once decorated the inner walls of the south porch have now almost vanished. In the north porch the paintings on the north wall are well-preserved, with ten complete scenes from the Old Testament, seven of which have been identified. The identifiable scenes are Jacob's dream, Jacob's struggle with the angels, Moses and the burning bush, Job in his suffering, the prophet Gideon, the tree of Jesse, and the hospitality of Abraham. One of the other three scenes depicts eight unidentified warrior saints, and a second shows Christ in the center of a group. In the western porch one fragmentary scene from the Old Testament survives, the Last Judgment, along with two portraits of saints.

The narthex contains portions of a very full cycle of scenes from the New Testament, all of them concerned with the miracles of Christ. It is roofed by a vault that springs from the sides at a low level, and is divided into three sectors by wide ribs. Both the northern and southern sectors contain five scenes separated near the middle by a decorative band. The central sector is in the form of a quadripartite groined vault, decorated along the junction with geometric designs and with two pairs each of seraphim and tetramorphs in the four quarters. The figurative paintings in the northern sector are: The deesis (Christ flanked by the Virgin and St. John the Baptist), the miracle of the loaves and fishes, Christ walking on the water and stilling the winds, and the healing of Peter's mother-in-law. Those in the southern sector are: the baptism of Christ, Christ cures the man born blind at the pool of Siloam, Christ discoursing with the doctors in the temple, the marriage feast at Cana, and the healing of the paralytic. The south wall of the narthex is decorated with three scenes: the casting out of a devil from the Canaanite woman's daughter; a miracle, perhaps the raising of Jairus' daughter; a fragmentary figure of Christ; and portraits of

SS. Sergius and Bacchus. Above the west door of the narthex is the mandelion, and on the arch the figures of St. Makarios and St. Poimen, with the remains of an unidentified sainted monk on the wall to the south. The upper portion of the north wall is occupied by the miracle of the loaves and fishes. The east wall contains the annunciation.

Within the nave of the church all or part of 25 scenes and 48 portraits have survived. The vault of the central apse displays the ascension and in the conch is the virgin enthroned between archangels. The dome is decorated with the figure of Christ Pantocrator, the Almighty, of which only the head and shoulders remain. Below this there is a long inscription containing the text of Psalm101:19, 20: "Out of the heavens did the Lord behold the earth, that he might hear the mournings of such as are in captivity and deliver the children appointed unto death that they might declare the name of the Lord in Sion and His worship in Jerusalem." Below the inscription there is a frieze of angels of surpassing beauty.

The other identifiable scene paintings on the upper surfaces and walls of the church include the washing of the feet, the Last Supper, the agony in the garden, the murder of Zacharias, the birth of the Virgin, the presentation of the Virgin in the temple, the meeting of Joachim and St. Anne, the annunciation to St. Anne, Joachim and St. Anne bring offerings, the prayer of St. Anne, the Nativity, the baptism with St. Mark, the Crucifixion with St. Matthew, the anastasis with St. John the Evangelist, the Apostles, the prophets, the judgment before Pilate, the denial of Peter, the Crucifixion, the Anastasis, the incredulity of Thomas, the appearance of Christ on the shores of the lake of Tiberias, and the mission of the Apostles. Among the identifiable portraits are representations of the two famous Stylites, or Pillar-Sitters, St. Simeon the Elder and St. Simeon the Younger, as well as those of St. Sabas, St. Anthony, St. Euthemios, St. Theodosios the Cenobiarch, St. Eleutherios, St. Gregory of Agrigento, St. Basil, St. Athanasios, and St. Epiphanios of Cyprus.

In the south apse, just beside the diaconicon, there is an unpaved area that was clearly the site of a tomb. It has been suggested that this was the burial place of Manuel I Comnenus, the founder of Haghia Sophia, who died in 1263.

Excavations just to the north of the north porch have uncovered the foundations of a small church. This had a roof or dome supported by two columns and two piers, its nave terminating to the east in three semicircular apses. This church is believed to predate Haghia Sophia, but no definite evidence has been found to establish its date of foundation.

We now make our way eastward toward the center of Trabzon along the main avenue. About a kilometer beyond Haghia Sophia we pass on our left the *türbe* of Pir Mehmet, dated 1523. Some 500 meters beyond this we come to Atatürk Parkı, where we see on our right Gülbahar Hatun Camii. This was built in 1505-06 by Prince Selim, the future Selim I, who dedicated the mosque to his mother Ayşe Hatun, also known as Gülbahar, the Rose of Spring. Gülbahar, a Greek girl of noble family whose original name was Maria Douberites, is buried in the splendid *türbe* beside the mosque.

At this point we might pause to look upon the walls of ancient and medieval Trebizond, as they rise up here just to the east of Atatürk Parkı. Here we might read the following description by Hamilton of Trebizond, which in his time was still separated from its suburbs by these walls and the two parallel ravines above which they were built:

> The situation of Trebizond is very remarkable; it is built at the foot of a high range of undulating hills, sloping gently to the beach, and everywhere well wooded....Beyond the low hills on which the town is built, and a little to the south-east, rises a steep and almost insulated hill, forming a perfectly level table-land, from which the town of Trapezus [in Greek "trapeza" means "table"] must have derived its name. It is now called Boz Tepe (grey hill)....
>
> The situation of the Turkish town is very picturesque, bounded to the east and west by rocky ravines of considerable depth, in all parts of

which are rich and luxuriant trees, and well-watered gardens; while the summits are fringed with the venerable and time-worn ruins of the Byzantine walls, which, with their numerous turrets and battlements, peep out above the mass of foliage which almost hides the rocky banks. This part of the town is connected with the suburbs by a high and narrow bridge on each side, and is defended by strongly-fortified gateways, above which, and entirely occupying the ground between the two ravines, are the extensive remains of an old and picturesque castle, the outer walls of which are of very great height. On one of its ivy-clad turrets we found two or three brass guns in a very ruinous state. The castle appears to be Byzantine, and was probably the palace of the Comneni, when they assumed the title of Emperors of Trebizond....Among its ruins, bays, laurels, and rhododendrons were growing in wild luxuriance.

The walled city is comprised of three tiered enceintes: the lower city, the middle city, and the upper city, the latter being the citadel. The citadel and the middle city are walled in along a long and

Trabzon, Medieval Byzantine Castle

narrow spur of rock defined by the two steep ravines that diverge below Boztepe, the Greek Mount Minthrion. This was the extent of Trebizond's fortifications up until the time of the Grand Comneni, who in the thirteenth century walled in the lower city. The lower city is twice as wide as the upper two enceintes, straddling the western ravine and extending down to the ancient port, whose harbor works were endowed by Hadrian in 129. During the time of the Grand Comneni Trebizond expanded along the shore eastward of the lower city as far as the much larger harbor of Daphnous, where the Venetians and Genoese had their fortresses and trading colonies around what has become the port of modern Trabzon.

Following the main avenue eastward from Atatürk Parkı, we pass the southwest corner of the medieval walls of the lower city, the only surviving gate of which is just to the left. We then cross the western ravine on Zaganos Köprüsü, a viaduct built by one of Fatih's generals, Zaganos Paşa, who erected it on foundations going back to Justinian's time. This brings us into the center of the middle city, where we come to the building known variously as Orta Cami or Fatih Camii. This is the former church of the Panayia Chrysokephalos, the Golden-Headed Virgin, which was converted to a mosque by Fatih immediately after his conquest of Trebizond in 1461.

The Panayia Chrysokephalos was the cathedral of Trebizond in the era of the Grand Comneni, most of whom were crowned here at the beginning of their reign and laid to rest here when their days were over. The edifice was rebuilt on a number of occasions in both the Byzantine and Ottoman periods. Thus in times past there was some confusion about the various stages of its structure, but a recent study by Selina Ballance has now clarified the architectural history of the Chrysokephalos.

Local tradition has it that the original church was founded in the fourth century, but there is no evidence to support this belief. An inscription, now lost, recorded that in 913-914 the Metropolitan Basil was restored to his episcopal throne in the Chrysokephalos, but there is no additional information on how long the church had been in existence at that time. The original church was replaced in the tenth or eleventh century by a completely new basilica. This basilica comprises the present building from apse to narthex, with the nave and side aisles arranged in six bays. There is a narthex that extends around three sides of the building, and galleries over the side aisles. A major reconstruction in the twelfth century involved raising the vault, constructing the crossing and a central dome, and adding the narthex. The north porch was added in the late thirteenth or early fourteenth century, as well as a chamber in the northeast corner. A south porch may also have been added at that time, but this was demolished and blocked off when the building was converted to a mosque. The Ionic columns and capitals in the north porch were reused from an ancient building. Then, finally, the south apse was added in the fourteenth or fifteenth century.

Wooden boards conceal the opus sectile floor and plaster obscures the wall paintings and the apse mosaic, the latter perhaps representing the Panayia Theotokos mentioned by travelers. Not a trace remains of the imperial funerary monuments of the Comneni dynasty, several of whom are known to have been buried in the Chrysokephalos.

We now continue on in the same direction until we come to the Hükümet Konağı, or Government House. Here we turn right on Kale Sokağı, which takes us through the middle city and up into the citadel, known in Turkish as İçkale. The upper city is now almost completely hemmed in by houses, through whose gardens we must wend our way in order to explore the Citadel and its walls. The only Muslim monument in the upper city is beside the lane that leads into the Citadel. This is İçkale Camii, also known as Şirin Hatun Camii. The little mosque was founded in 1470 by Şehzade Abdullah, a son of Beyazit II, who dedicated it to his mother Şirin Hatun. The dedicatory inscription is on the fountain at the northwest corner of the mosque.

The fortifications in the citadel date back to Classical times, with extensive rebuilding and strengthening of the defenses by the Grand Comneni. The famous "Golden Palace" of the Comneni was located in the southwestern quarter of the upper city, while the open courtyard known as the Epiphaneia was at its southern apex, where John IV built a huge defense tower, completing it in 1458, five years after the fall of Constantinople and three years before Trebizond fell to the Turks. An old Pontic folk song tells of how news of the fall of Constantinople, the great City, reached Trebizond, where the Byzantine Empire was known as Romania, the realm of Rome in the East:

A bird, a good bird, left the City,
it settled neither in vineyards nor in orchards,
it came to settle on the castle of the Sun.
it shook one wing, drenched in blood,
it shook the other wing, it had a written paper.
Now it reads, now it cries, now it beats its breast.
"Woe is us, woe is us, Romania is taken."
The churches lament, the monasteries weep.
And St. John Chrysostom weeps, he beats his breast.
Weep not, weep not, St. John, and beat not your breast.
Romania has passed away, Romania is taken.
Even if Romania has passed away, it will flower and bear fruit again.

We now return to the Hükümet Konağı, where we turn right to follow the main street as it approaches the eastern ravine. As we do so we pass on our right a huge and ornate building in Italianate style, dating from the early twentieth century. This is the Trabzon Müze Binası, which is now being restored to house the Trabzon Museum.

We now cross the eastern ravine on Tabakhane Köprüsü, leaving the middle city. This viaduct is also erected on ancient foundations, rebuilt on several occasions in both the Byzantine and Ottoman periods. After crossing the bridge we take the first narrow street on our left. This brings us to Küçük Ayvasil Kilisesi, which is probably the oldest church surviving from Byzantine Trebizond.

The Turkish name of this ancient edifice means the Little Church of St. Basil, so called because it stood not far from a larger church dedicated to the same saint, now vanished, though Küçük Ayvasil Kilisesi was actually dedicated to St. Anne. A relief slab over the door bears an inscription recording that the church was restored in 884-85, during the reign of the Byzantine emperor Basil I and his two sons, Leo IV and Alexander, who were then ruling with him as co-emperors. The relief, which was taken from an unidentified ancient building, depicts an armed warrior and an angel in flight. Two Ionic capitals in the church were also reused from ancient structures. St. Anne's seems to have served as a mortuary chapel for court officials and high-ranking clerics, seven of whom were identified by inscribed portraits that were once visible in the church, their dates ranging from 1361 to 1413. The church was also decorated with scenes from the cycle of SS. Joachim and Anne, of which their dormition has survived. St. Anne's continued to serve as a church up until 1923; unfortunately it is now closed to the public.

After passing the church we emerge on Maraş Caddesi, the main east-west avenue of Trabzon. After crossing the avenue we continue straight ahead, entering the labyrinthine market quarter, which extends eastward along the shore from the lower city. There are a number of monuments in this quarter and in the lower city from both the Byzantine and Ottoman periods, but it is impossible to give precise directions on how to find them in this maze, and so one must ask the local merchants, who are always willing to help.

The oldest of the Ottoman buildings in this quarter is the Bedesten, which is believed to have been founded by the future Selim I when he was governor of Trabzon in the years 1489-1512. The second oldest is Taşhan, also known as Vakıfhan, a two-storied caravanserai built in 1531 by İskender Paşa, who succeeded Prince Selim as governor of Trabzon in 1512. İskender Paşa also built the mosque that bears his name near the new port on the eastern side of town.

Other Turkish buildings in Trabzon include: Çifte Hamam (probably a medieval church in origin, converted to a public bath soon after the Conquest), Sekiz Direkli Hamam (supposedly a Selçuk bath dating from the late Byzantine period, abandoned until 1988, when it was restored and reopened for public use), Paşa Hamamı (early sixteenth century), İskenderpaşa Çeşmeleri (two fountains by the same donor, one dated 1520 and the other 1523), Şadırvan (a reservoir centered on an hexagonal water tank supported by six columns, traditionally dated to the sixteenth century and restored in 1963); Erdoğdu Bey Camii (1522, heavily restored), Hacı Kasım Camii (1531), Semerciler Camii (1579, restored in 1820, the only old mosque in Trabzon with a painted wooden ceiling), Tekke Camii (1591, a dervish *tekke* converted to a mosque), Kalkanoğlu Hoca Halil Camii (sixteenth century, restored in the nineteenth century), Musa Paşa Camii (1668), Yarımbıyıkoğlu Konağı (1706), Kundupoğlu Konağı (early eighteenth century), Alacahan (eighteenth century), and Çarşı Camii (1879).

Among the other Byzantine churches converted to mosques after the conquest, the most important is Yeni Cuma Camii, the New Friday Mosque, which is 200 meters to the east of the citadel and on the opposite side of the eastern ravine. This is the former monastic church of St. Eugenios, dedicated to the patron saint of Trebizond. The original church was founded by the Byzantine emperor Basil II in 1021-22, while he was on campaign in northeastern Asia Minor and the Caucasus. It was rebuilt in 1291 and again after 1340 by the Grand Comneni, whose imperial portraits are among the many wall paintings and mosaics now covered up by plaster. Alexius III was crowned in St. Eugenios on 21 January 1340, probably because the Chrysokephalos was then under repair. The building has a cruciform plan, with a dome on a high drum over the crossing, terminating at the east in an apse that is semicircular within and five-sided on the exterior.

The prominent position of the church on a hilltop across the ravine from the citadel made it a strategic point in a number of sieges of Trebizond, both in civil wars and in attacks by invading armies. In 1223 it was taken by the Selçuks when they attacked Trebizond under Mugisettin Tuğrul Şah, son of Sultan Kılıçarslan II, better known as Melik. Melik set up his camp on the hill close to St. Eugenios, and after his first assault on the citadel failed he threatened to burn down the church. When he began his second assault the abbot of the monastery displayed on the walls of the citadel the most sacred relic of the church, a reliquary containing the head of St. Eugenios, and this drove off the attackers, according to a Byzantine chronicler. But St. Eugenios could not help Trebizond in 1461, when David II surrendered the city to Fatih after a siege of six weeks. Fatih immediately converted the church into a mosque and attended the first Muslim service there on the Friday after the Conquest, hence the name Yeni Cuma Camii. According to his Greek biographer, Kritovoulos of Imbros, Fatih went directly from the newly converted mosque to make his first inspection of the upper city: "He ascended to the citadel and the palace, and saw and admired the security of the one and the splendor of the other, and in every way he judged the city worthy of note."

Other Byzantine churches of Trebizond that were converted to mosques are: Nakip Camii (dated tenth to twelfth century, possibly dedicated to St. Andrew); Kindinar Camii (church of St. Akindynos, earlier than the twelfth century), Kudreteyn Camii (church of St. Philip, fourteenth-century), Zeytinlik Camii, and Küçük Fatih Camii. The thirteenth-century church of St. John the Sanctifier, which was completely rebuilt in 1895, is now part of the Kaledibi Primary School in the Hızırbey district, where it is used as an exhibition gallery.

The impressive remains of the most important convent of Byzantine Trebizond can be seen on the northwest spur of Boz Tepe, ancient Mount Minthrion, the great table-hill that towers above the city to the southeast. Known in Turkish as Kızlar Manastırı, the Monastery of the Girls, it was founded in the 1340s and dedicated to the Panayia Theoskepastos, the God-Protected Virgin, with a huge endowment that made it one of the richest convents in the empire of Trebizond. The Grand Comnenus Manuel III (1390-1427) was laid to rest in the Theoskepastos in 1417; and twelve years later Alexius IV was buried there, though he was later reinterred in a tomb beside the Chrysokephalos. Among the many wall paintings that probably still survive under the plaster in the conventual church is one, described by several travelers, representing three imperial figures. An inscription identifies these as Alexius II, his wife Theodora Cantacuzena, and his mother Eirene, who is shown holding a model of the church. This has led to the conclusion that Eirene was the founder of the Theoskepastos, which continued to function as a convent until 1923. The church is built in a cave with a sacred spring, which tradition says was once a shrine of Mithras, the Persian sun god from whom Mount Minthrion took its name. Tradition also has it that there was a colossal statue of Mithras that stood in his shrine on this mountain. The tradition goes on to say that during the reign of Diocletian the statue was toppled by St. Eugenios and his followers, who as a result suffered martyrdom.

Five hundred meters farther to the east there is another cave-sanctuary on the northern face of Boztepe, this one dedicated to St. Sabas. There are actually three rock-cut chapels in the complex, two of which have been dated to the second half of the thirteenth century and the third to 1411, as evidenced by an inscription.

Some seven kilometers southwest of Atatürk Parkı, indicated by road signs, there is a handsome mansion now known as the Atatürk Pavilion. This was built in 1903 by a wealthy Greek named Constantine Kubayanides; during the years 1916-17 it served as the headquarters of the Russian forces then occupying Trabzon. After the founding of the Turkish Republic it became state property, and when Atatürk visited Trabzon on 15 September 1924 it was presented to him as a gift. Atatürk stayed there during visits to Trabzon in 1930 and 1937, and after his death in 1938 it passed to his sister Makbule Atadan. The building reverted to the state in 1943; and in 1964 it was converted into a museum, furnished in the style of the early Republic and exhibiting memorabilia of Atatürk's visits to Trabzon.

One might conclude a visit to Trabzon by taking a last stroll through the medieval quarter in the upper city, which still retains some haunting memories of its illustrious past. Walking along these narrow, winding lanes, under the walls of the Golden Palace of the Grand Comneni, one inevitably recalls the elegiac lines with which

Rose Macaulay ended her novel, *The Towers of Trebizond:*

Still the towers of Trebizond, the fabled city, shimmer on a far horizon, gated and walled and held in a luminous enchantment. It seems for me, and however much I stand outside them, this must forever be. But at the city's heart lies the pattern and the hard core, and this I can never make my own: they are too far outside my range.

CHAPTER SEVEN

SOUTH AND EAST OF TRABZON

Our next itinerary will take us east of Trabzon to the Georgian border, with excursions south into the Pontic Alps. Our first excursion will take us south from Trabzon to visit the famous monastery of Soumela, starting out on highway E97.

The first part of our route takes us up the valley of the Değirmendere, the river which in antiquity was called the Pyxitis, with its upper course known as the Prytanis. The region through which the river flowed was known to the Greeks as the Matzouka, which gave its name to the fierce mountaineers whose Greek-speaking Muslim descendents still live in some of these valleys. The Matzouka was the heartland of the Empire of Trebizond, as evidenced by the numerous churches and monasteries that one sees in the area, as well as the watchtowers and fortresses built to defend this main approach from the Anatolian plateau to the coast. The highway along which we drive out of Trabzon was the first stretch of the ancient caravan route between the Euxine and Persia via Erzurum, and today it is once again the principal route between the Black Sea and Iran.

After passing Boztepe, the table-hill behind Trabzon, the highway takes us up the lush valley of the Değirmendere, whose stream is spanned in several places by ancient hog-backed bridges that were once part of the old caravan road, some of them in more remote areas still covered with wooden roofs. Hamilton mentions some of these bridges in his description of his trip south from Trebizond along the valley of the Surmel, a stream just to the east of the Değirmendere. His graphic description that follows illustrates the great difficulties of travelling through the Pontic Alps in the days before the first modern paved highways were laid down, the hardships of the journey perhaps alleviated by the surpassing beauty of the lush mountain scenery:

We started at 9 A.M., ascending the steep hills to the S. and S.S.E. of the town, the view of which as we looked back was highly picturesque. On reaching the summit of the ridge I found the yellow Azalea Pontica and the purple Rhododendron in full flower, growing wild with great luxuriance, the former scenting the air with its sweet perfume....

The traffic on this line, which is the caravan road from Trebizond to Erzeroum, is always considerable; but, owing to the nature of the soil, and the heavy rains which fall all the year round near the sea, it is so cut up and poached by long trains of beasts of burden, as to be often impassable. To obviate this evil in part, a narrow paved causeway has beeen laid down in many places, where the nature of the ground required it most, but the lapse of years has reduced it to a most wretched state; and what between floundering in the mud on one side or the other, and slipping about on the broken uneven pavement, the baggage horses had great difficulty in getting along. Between five and six miles from Trebizond we reached the bed of the Surmel, and ascended the wooded and well-cultivated valley for several miles. Our direction here changed to S.S.W., and three miles farther on we passed a small village consisting, like most others up this road, of blacksmiths and bakers, for the convenience of caravans. At this village a small bridge, covered with a wooden roof, crosses the Surmel immediately above which another stream falls into it from a more beautiful valley to the S.S.E.

At a quarter after one a stone bridge carried us across the Surmel, a deep torrent flowing through igneous rocks... we quitted the bottom of the valley, ascending the wooded hills on our left, while on the other side was the chiftlik [large farm] of a Turkish Agha, an independent country gentleman, once a Dere Bey, whose house was picturesquely situated on the summit of a wooded knoll commanding an extensive view of the valley. For three miles we ascended the hills, partly cultivated and partly wooded, until we reached the summit of the ridge which separates the two valleys above mentioned, of which that to the west is called Matchka and that to the east Meremana. For nearly three miles our road led along the crest, through the most beautiful scenery that can be imagined, and between thick woods of beech and fir, under which azaleas and rhododendron, covered with a profusion of fragrant flowers, formed an impenetrable and luxuriant underwood, while the eye wandered over extensive hills and deeply secluded valleys to the left, the summits of which were crowned with woods, while their sides were cultivated, wherever it was possible. Nature here appeared in one of her most fascinating garbs. As we advanced the azaleas increased in number and size, and the whole scene rather resembled a garden or beautiful shrubbery than a mountain in its native wildness....

The first caravan stop coming up from the Black Sea was Maçka, the ancient Dikaisimon, which is now 28 kilometers from Trabzon on the highway. Maçka preserves in corrupted form the ancient name of the region—Matzouka—of which Dikaisimon was the administrative center in Byzantine times. Local tradition among the Greeks was that the Grand Comneni had a summer palace in Dikaisimon, though no trace of this has ever been found. At the time of the population exchange in 1923 three quarters of the population of Maçka were Greek, all of whom were supposedly deported. But many people in Maçka and its surrounding area still speak Greek, though they are all Muslims, indicating that they converted to Islam at some point in the past.

There are remains of numerous Byzantine churches in the immediate vicinity of Maçka, many of them with wall paintings dating from the medieval era, though all of them are now in ruins. One of the most notable of these is Sarmaşıklı Kilise, the "Ivy Church," whose extensive and well-preserved paintings have been recorded by David Winfield, who has dated the building to the late fourteenth or early fifteenth century. But here as elsewhere the paintings are fast disappearing, many of them destroyed by vandals, and some by religious zealots as opposed to figurative representations as the iconoclasts of medieval Byzantium. Bryer and Winfield note a dramatic example of such iconoclasm in connection with their description of a picture of St. Theodore Stratilates in Sarmaşıklı Kilise:

There was rather more left of St. Theodore when D.C.W. [Winfield] first visited the church, but here inspection of the paintings was frequently interrupted by an old crone. She regularly came to peer at him over the south aisle, whence she hurled imprecations. On her final visit of the day she appeared brandishing an adze, which D.C.W. greatly feared was intended for him and his wife, but she was diverted from rushing at them by St. Theodore, whose image she attacked with great vigor. There is no fury like that of an iconoclast unleashed, and they fled.

The most famous of the monasteries both in the days of the Grand Comneni and today is Soumela, which is approached by a turnoff to the left from Maçka, following the signpost for Meryemana Manastırı. This takes us up the valley of the Panayia Suyu, the Stream of the Virgin, known in antiquity as the Galianos. As we begin the drive we pass within sight of a hilltop ruin on the left— Doubera Kale—one of the watchtowers built by the Grand Comneni along this route. This may be the castle mentioned by Alexius III, in an order enjoining the Soumela monastery to hold this point against the Turks. There are two chapels within the fortress; one of them, dedicated to St. John the Baptist, has been dated to the late thirteenth or early fourteenth century.

The fortress takes its name from the village of Doubera, now known as Yazlık, which stands high above the eastern cliffs of the Panayia Suyu some six kilometers south-southeast of Maçka. Doubera was one of the principal communities of the Matzouka during the days of the Grand Comneni. This was where Theodore, commander-in-chief of the Trapezuntine army (i.e., army of Trebizond) under the emperor Andronicus I Gidon, captured and held Melik after the unsuccessful Turkish siege of Trebizond in 1223. Doubera was the birthplace of Maria Douberites, later to become Gülbahar Hatun, wife of Beyazit I and mother of Selim I, whose mosque and *türbe* we have seen in Trabzon.

The valley of the Panayia Suyu is even more scenic than that of the Değirmendere. Travelers to Soumela have long sung the praises of this valley, perhaps the most eloquent being the historian George

Finlay, who passed this way in 1850. As he wrote in his diary: "It is impossible not to be in ecstasy over such scenery. It offers the precipices of Etolia and the waters of Switzerland and the richest vegetation of Brusa mingled with the flowers of Damascus."

We round the last bend in the road and suddenly Soumela comes into view, an enormous pink-and-white monastery clinging to the cliff face of Melas, the Black Mountain, more than 300 meters above the rushing stream in the valley below, looking like a Tibetan hermitage from the set of *Lost Horizon*. Here again we refer to Finlay, who evokes a picture of what the approach to Soumela was like when the crowds approaching it were pilgrims rather than tourists, and when the monastery was inhabited by monks instead of ghosts. In his enthusiasm he more than triples the elevation of the monastery:

> The roar of the waters more than 3,000 feet below the monastery, the snowy slopes visible on the ridge over the valley which is hardly a rifle-shot across, the immense wooden pile of buildings with its galleries and cells clinging like swallows' nests to the precipice, the sound of the convent bell continually announcing the arrival of parties of pilgrims and the nasal chant of the continual masses was grand, solemn and picturesque.

According to tradition, the original shrine here was founded in 385 by two monks from Athens, Barnabas and his brother Sophronius. One night the Virgin appeared to Barnabas in a dream and told him to go to the Pontus and built a shrine for her icon, which portrayed her as the Panayia Atheniotissa, Our Lady of Athens, also known as the Gorgoepikos, "the one who answers requests quickly." The Virgin told Barnabas that she had lost patience with the Athenians because of their pagan ways, and so she was removing her icon from Athens and sending it to the Pontus. When Barnabas and Sophronius looked for the icon in the Virgin's church in Athens they found that the sacred picture had disappeared, and so they went off to the Pontus in search of it. After a long search

Soumela Monastery, Distant View

they finally found the icon in a cave high on the Black Mountain, with a spring of life-giving water gushing from within the grotto. Thereupon they built a chapel within the cave and enshrined the icon there, calling it the Panayia tou Melas, the Virgin of the Black Rock, which in the Pontic dialect soon became known as Soumela. Tradition goes on to say that a monastery was established at Soumela in the first half of the fifth century, during the reign of Theodosius II, and that it was rebuilt on a larger scale in the following century by Belisarius, Justinian's great general. But there is no evidence to support this belief, and it appears that the monastery was not established until the tenth century. In any event, the greatest period in the history of Soumela was during the days of the Empire of Trebizond, when it enjoyed the patronage of several of the Grand Comneni, including John II (r. 1280-97), Alexius II (r. 1297-1330), Basil II (r. 1332-40), and Alexius III (r. 1349-90), who in 1364 issued a chrysobull, or imperial edict, exempting the monastery from all taxes and restrictions as well as granting it extensive estates in the Matzouka. Soumela continued to flourish in the Ottoman period, with Selim I confirming the rights and privileges that had been granted by the Grand Comneni and also presenting to the monastery two enormous silver candlesticks, which were still shown to visitors as late as 1896. Soumela remained in existence as a monastery up until 1923, when it was abandoned after its monks were deported in the population exchange. Soon afterwards it was ravaged by a fire, and in the following half century it suffered further damage from the elements and vandals. A program of preservation was begun in the 1970s; and now, though the monastery is completely in ruins, its surviving structures and frescoes are protected from further damage.

A winding path leads up from the entrance of the site by the river, a steep hike of about forty-five minutes that takes one up through the dense greenery with ever expanding views of the heavily forested valley, and with the sound of the rushing torrent far below growing gradually fainter.

The monastic buildings are laid out around three sides of a long

Soumela Monastery, Interior

and narrow rectangular ledge, the fourth and back side of which is formed by the sheer cliff of Mount Melas. The only entrance is at the south end, where a long stairway leads up past the arches of an aqueduct dating from the Ottoman period. Just inside the entrance are the quarters once used by the hegumenos, or guestmaster, who in times past would welcome the visitor with a glass of raki and a plate of goat cheese and olives, just as monks do today in the monasteries of Mount Athos in Greece. (The last entry in the Soumela guest book, now in Greece, that visitors signed when they entered the monastery here bears the date 24 June 1921.) There is a small court two meters below this to the north. The main court lies some 15 meters below this, approached by another long stairway. The main court is bordered on its eastern side by the main living rooms of the monks and the quarters for their guests. These rooms continue along the east side of the courtyard, while on the west side is the library and the cave church, with the apse and nave of a chapel projecting from the wall that closes in part of the cavern. There are additional dormitories to the northeast, along with three chapels. North of the main court the outside buildings continue for more than 25 meters along a narrower part of the ledge, their outer walls separated from the edge of the precipice by nothing more than a narrow verandah.

The cave church and the frescoes that originally decorated its walls date from 1710, when the monastery was almost completely restored; and the present frescoes date from a redecoration ca. 1740. The cave church itself is far older, probably dating from a reconstruction by Alexius III in the years 1350-65. The chronicler Panaretos records an incident that occurred in the second year of that period:

> ...on Wednesday 5 May 1351, at the fifth hour, there was an eclipse of the sun, such as had not been witnessed in all our lifetime, so that the stars shown in the sky and it lasted one-and-one-half hours. Lord Alexius the Emperor and Lady Eirene his mother were found congregated in the monastery of Soumela in Matzouka, making many

Soumela Monastery, Cave Church

prayers and supplications.

Many of the surviving paintings have been defaced by modern graffiti, but beneath these there are inscriptions from the days of the Grand Comneni, including the following one in the ruined library: "Repeat thee not the flow of my tears. With the light of thy radiance thy shineth, Virgin, dispelling the darkness of my ignorance."

Beside the projecting apse of the chapel in the cave church there is a springhouse opening on to the courtyard. This encloses the sacred spring of the Virgin, where many visitors pause to make wishes just as pilgrims did in times past.

Soumela was the most renowned of the three great monasteries of the Matzouka. The other two were Vazelon, dedicated to St. John the Baptist, and Peristera, dedicated to St. George. Vazelon is ten kilometers to the south-southwest of Maçka and Peristera ten kilometers to the southeast, both now accessible by road. Vazelon and Peristera were founded at about the same time as Soumela, and both also had extensive estates in the Matzouka. They are both in ruins, but nevertheless impressive, preserving some fragments of their wall paintings; and are well worth a visit for those travelers who have the time.

We now retrace our route to Trabzon, after which we resume our journey eastward along the Black Sea coast.

Driving out of Trabzon we cross the mouth of the Değirmendere. Just to the east of Trabzon's port a small headland marks the site of one of the lost churches of Byzantine Trebizond, that of St. Blaisios. This medieval church was still standing in 1879, but it has long since disappeared, perhaps destroyed during World War I or its aftermath. The earliest mention of St. Blaisios is by the French traveler Bordier, who visited the church in 1609, reporting that he saw displayed in the nave a ship's pennant with the arms of England. This would have been the pennant of the *Royall Defence,* for which Sir Thomas Glover in 1609 obtained from the Sublime Porte a firman, or imperial decree, entitling him to sail his vessel in the Euxine, the "first English shippe that ever swome in these seas."

Continuing eastward along highway 010, the first place of interest that we pass is Araklı, the ancient Heracleia, a drive of 39 kilometers from Trabzon. Unlike a number of other ancient towns of this name, Heracleia was not named after the god Heracles but the emperor Heraclonas. Heraclonas was born here in 626 to the empress Martina while his father, the emperor Heraclius, was on campaign against the Persians. Heraclonas and his elder brother, Constantine II, ruled briefly as co-emperors after Heraclius died on 11 February 641. Constantine died of consumption on 28 May of that year; and at the end of September Heraclonas was deposed, mutilated and exiled, ending two of the shortest reigns in Byzantine history. At Araklı there is a ruined Byzantine fortress known as Kalecik, built by the Grand Comneni of Trebizond, and also the remains of a fortified Roman encampment named Canayer. Canayer was undoubtedly where Heraclius was camped with his army when his wife Martina gave birth to the unfortunate Heraclonas, who was never heard from again after his early downfall, though his name is perpetuated here in Araklı.

Seven kilometers beyond Araklı we pass Sürmene, the ancient Sourmaina, where there is another ruined Byzantine fortress dating from the time of the Grand Comneni. Five kilometers farther along we come to Sürmene Kastil, where we see the finest surviving Ottoman mansion on the Black Sea coast of Turkey, the Memiş Ağa Yakupoğlu Konağı, dating from the late eighteenth century. The leader of the Yakupoğlu clan was the local *derebey*, or lord of the valley, one of the feudal leaders who continued to hold power in eastern Anatolia up until late Ottoman times. The Yakupoğlu family continued to live in the *konak* in Sürmene Kastil up until the 1970s, but they have now moved into more modern housing.

About nine kilometers beyond Sürmene Kastil we pass a ruined Byzantine fortress known as Roşi Kalesi, after which we come to the village of Of, the ancient Ophis. The villagers here, the Oflu,

Sürmeli Kastil, Memiş Ağa Yakupoğlu Konağı

are Greek-speaking Muslims, as are the majority of those living to
the south of them in the valley of the Solaklı Çayı, most notably in
the town of Çaykara. This and the areas around Tonya and Maçka
are among the very few Greek-speaking pockets left in Anatolia.
Another Greek-speaking group, the Santaioi, inhabit a group of
eight villages in the valley of the Yanbolu, the river known to the
Greeks as the Santa, which flows into the sea just to the east of
Araklı. As with the people of Tonya and Maçka, the Oflu and the
Santaioi are undoubtedly descended from Pontic Greeks who
converted to Islam after the Turkish Conquest. (A census in the late
fifteenth century showed that the population of the Rize district, in
which Of is included, had 2,063 Christian households and only 162
that were Muslim, indicating that the mass conversion to Islam had
not yet begun by then.) These people speak Greek only among
themselves, otherwise using Turkish. Despite their Greek speech
(or perhaps because of it), the Oflu are known as staunch and pious
Muslims, and many of the older men, bearded sages of Biblical

aspect, have made the pilgrimage to Mecca, as evidenced by their green skull-caps, although one still hears tales of crypto-Christians here and elsewhere in the Pontus.

Here we make an excursion south on highway 915, which will take us up through the Pontic mountains along the valley of the Solaklı Çayı. Our first destination is Uzungöl, which is up the valley of a tributary river of the Solaklı Çayı on a very rough road, so those traveling in ordinary cars are advised to park in Çaykara and take a minibus from there. The scenery en route is wild and beautiful, as the road winds along the bank of the Solaklı and its tributary, passing a number of ancient hog-backed stone bridges as well as covered wooden spans, dating back to the mid-eighteenth century.

The road ends at Uzungöl, a little village at the end of a long and narrow lake of picture-postcard prettiness. The lake is at an altitude of 1,250 meters, ringed by the towering peaks of Mt. Ziyaret (3,111 meters) and Mt. Haldizen (3,193 meters). The lakeside village, known as Şerali, is a rustic hamlet of well-made wooden cottages, with the outlying houses set higher up on the verdant slopes of the encircling mountains, each surrounded by its *yayla,* or highland meadow, a characteristic scene in the Pontic Alps. Here as in the other villages south of Of, many of the locals are Greek-speakers, though pious Muslims.

Returning to the main valley of the Solaklı Çayı, at the road junction one can turn south on highway 915 to visit Zil Kalesi, a drive of about half an hour. Although in ruins, Zil Kalesi is still a very impressive sight, its shattered towers rising like spires from a crag at least 100 meters above the river as it passes through a narrow gorge. The fortress consisted of an outer bailey, which may have extended down as far as the river, a middle bailey, and a keep on the uppermost level. Zil Kalesi dates from the late Byzantine period, but it may have been built by a local warlord rather than the Grand Comneni.

We now make our way back to Of, where we resume our journey eastward along the coast.

Some 24 kilometers beyond Of we arrive at Rize, the largest town on the Black Sea coast of Turkey east of Trabzon. Rize is the ancient Rhizaion, whose site was on the promontory east of the modern town, where we see the ruins of its medieval castle. This fortress was originally erected by Justinian, and it was later rebuilt and strengthened by the Grand Comneni of Trebizond. Procopius writes of this fortress in his *Edifices,* an account of all the structures that Justinian erected throughout the Byzantine Empire during his reign. He notes that Justinian "restored Rhizaion himself, throwing about it a novel system of defenses which surpass any description or report of them. For it was fashioned to be inferior in point of size and security to not one of the cities on the Persian frontier."

Rize is the capital of the tea-growing region on the Turkish Black Sea coast. This is evidenced by the tea plantations that one sees rising up the mountainside tier upon tier as one drives along the coast, and by the harvested leaves drying outside the local houses before being processed in the tea factories in and around Rize. Its tea plantations and hazelnut groves are important to the province of Rize. While in Rize travelers should avail themselves of the opportunity to visit a tea factory and learn something about how these glossy green leaves are transformed into the dry, black fragments that we think of as tea. The principal sight in Rize is the Tea Institute, a research center that has both a botanical garden open to visitors and a teahouse.

Continuing eastward, about ten kilometers out of town we pass a ruined Byzantine fortress called Bozukkale; and then, 23 kilometers from Rize, we come to Çayeli. This is the site of ancient Mavpari, the last major settlement of the Greeks of the Trapezuntine Empire (i.e., the empire of Trebizond) in this direction, for east of here one entered Lazia, the land of the Laz, the Caucasian people who still predominate in this region today.

A short way farther along we cross the Kalecik Deresi, whose headland was graced until recent years by a ruined Byzantine fortress named Sivrikale, but this has since been destroyed in road-

Rize

Rize, View of the Acropolis Fortress

building operations. Sivrikale was the citadel of ancient Kordyla, a stronghold of the Grand Comneni that for a time marked the border between the Trapezuntine Empire and Lazia, the Kingdom of the Laz.

Five kilometers beyond Kalecik Deresi we come to Pazar, which in antiquity was known as Athenai. Despite its name, Athenai had no historical associations with ancient Athena, though it was undoubtedly an ancient Greek colony. The original site of Athenai is marked by a romantic ruin that stands on a seagirt promontory about a kilometer west of Pazar, a castle known as Kız Kulesi, the Maiden's Tower. Here as elsewhere along the coast, the castle dates from the time of the Grand Comneni of Trebizond.

Pazar and the next four townships to its east—Ardeşen, Fındıklı, Arhavi, and Hopa—are almost exclusively Laz in population, and together they make up the largest Laz-speaking area in Turkey. One notices the Laz immediately in driving east from Pazar to Hopa, for many of them have red or blonde hair and blue or green eyes, the women free of veils and shawls and wearing knee-length skirts and short sleeves when working in the tea plantations, the aquiline-nosed men sporting elaborate moustaches and often carrying their pet hawks about with them, for hawking is still a very popular pastime here. The Laz have their own distinctive culture and character; and they are renowned throughout Turkey for their resourcefulness and sense of humor. They are also renouned for just being different, a fact that has made them the butt of numerous jokes. The Laz even tell Laz jokes about themselves: as the mayor of Ardeşen has said, with his pet hawk perched on his shoulder: "The only reason that we continue to speak Laz, is that in no other language can one tell so many hilarious jokes." Sevan Nişanyan has this to say about the Laz and Laz jokes in his book on the Black Sea region:

Predictably the Black Sea man, or the "Laz" as he is called with a mixture of affection and sneer, has become a stock figure of the Turkish social typology. The stereotypical Laz is called either Temel or Dursun. He sports a majestic nose and speaks Turkish with an outrageous accent. His diet consists of hamsi (Black Sea anchovies), cooked to the legendary one hundred recipes that include hamsi bread and hamsi jam, with corn bread and dark cabbage to accompany. He dances a wild horon to the syncopated manic tunes of a kemence [a stringed instrument similar to the Cretan lyre].

His oddball sense of humor makes him the butt of an entire genre of jokes. To a certain extent these jokes correspond to those of the Polish, Scottish, Marseillian or Basque variety, but they lack the crude ridicule that characterizes some of the latter. In most stories Temel either pursues an altogether wacky idea, or responds to situations with an insane non sequitur. The best ones contain a hint of self-mockery, and it is not really clear who the joke is on. Inevitably the most brilliant Laz jokes are circulated by the Laz themselves.

Along the coast between Pazar and Hopa the landscape is dominated by the majestic Kaçkar Mountains, whose highest peak is 3,937 meters above sea level and heavily forested right up to the snow line. They are one of several ranges that together make up the Pontic Alps, the mountain barrier that separates Asia Minor from the Caucasus, forming the bastion that for centuries protected the Trapezuntine coast from the invading armies that rode westward across the great Anatolian plateau.

Five kilometers beyond Pazar the coastal highway crosses the torrential Fırtına river, whose very name means "storm," in both Turkish and Greek. The Fırtına originates high in the Kaçkar Mountains, its valley providing one of the few avenues into the Pontic Alps from the Trapezuntine coast. Highway 53-05 leads from the coast up the Fırtına valley to the very Alpine village of Çamlıhemşin, a drive of 24 kilometers. This is one of the most beautiful of all the Pontic villages, its houses of stone and wood perched precariously on the mountainside above the thundering Fırtına river, the outlying homes being set in emerald green *yayla*s on the steeply sloping mountainsides. The villagers of Çamlıhemşin and the other communities of the Fırtına valley are not Laz but a people known in Turkish as the Hemşinli, their language a survival of the Armenian that their ancestors spoke before converting to Islam. Bryer and Winfield write thus of the Hemşinli:

> In the mountains behind Pazar and Ardeşen lurk the Hemşinli, who, after the Santaioi and the Oflus are the third of the peculiar people of the Pontic interior—peculiar even in a Laz context. The Hemşinli are not mentioned in any Trapezuntine source, but their *locus classicus* is Clavijo's account of his journey from İspir to the bandon [region] of Sourmaina in September 1405, when their exchange of their own Armenian lord Arhakel (a common Armenian name meaning "apostle") for a Muslim atabeğ might be regarded as a microcosm of Armenian history.

Clavijo's account of his journey gives a vivid picture of the world of the Pontic Alps in the last half century of the Byzantine period, describing a way of life that in some ways, particularly in modes of transport, is still much the same today in highland villages like Çamlıhemşin. He writes as follows about the Çamlıhemşin region, which he calls Arhakel:

> The Muslim lord of İspir city and district is also lord of the Arhakel (Arraquiel) district, and he has come to be so after this fashion. The men of the Arhakel district in the past became discontented with their lord, who bore the name Arhakel, like the district that was his. These folk therefore sent privily to that native lord of İspir, with whom they compassed to betray their master, promising that he, of İspir, should be made their ruler in the other's place. And so it fell out, for they delivered up Arhakel to the lord of İspir, whom he imprisoned, setting in his place to rule the Arhakel lands a Muslim governor, but at the same time appointing a Christian lord-deputy, to act as his assistant. All this countryside of Arhakel is very mountainous, with mere pathways that cross the passes, and these so rocky and steep that burdened horses cannot travel them. In some places they have to cut bridges of beams from rock to rock to traverse the hill crests. No

sumpter beasts are here in use, but men who are porters have to carry all the burdens on their shoulders. There is but little corn grown in this region, and the people are of a barbarous race. As we passed through we were in some danger from them, for though they are Armenians and profess to be Christians all are robbers and brigands; indeed they forced us, before we were let free to pass, to give a present of our goods as toll for the right of passage. We were four days journeying through their country and then came to the sea-shore....

The English traveler George Purchas (ca. 1577-1666) heard of, but did not visit, Çamlıhemşin, giving this fabulous description of the region in his account of "Armenia Major and Georgia" in *Purchas, His Pilgrimage,* published in London in 1614:

...in this kingdome is a thing monstrous and wonderfull, which I would not have spoken of or beleeved, had I not seen it with mine owne eyes. In these parts there is a Province called Hamseem, contayning in circuit three days journey; and so farre it is covered with an obscure

Çamlıhemşin

darkness, that none can see any thing, nor dare enter into it. The inhabitants thereabouts affirm, that they have often heard the voyce of men howling, cockes crowing, neighing of horses; and by the passage of a River, it appeareth to have signs of habitation. This is reported by the Armenian historians to have come to passe by the hand of God, so delivering his Christian servants, and so punishing with outward darkness the inward former blindness and rage of these persecuting idolaters.

We now return to the coastal highway and continue on to Hopa, a drive of 46 kilometers from the Çamlıhemşin turnoff.

Hopa is the easternmost town on the Black Sea coast of Turkey, the last port of call for ships of the Turkish Maritime Lines. During the days of the Grand Comneni it was known as Kissa, of which nothing now remains other than the ruins of a fortress.

The coastal highway continues on to the border post of Sarp on the boundary of Turkey and Georgia, a drive of 22 kilometers. The actual border on the coast is a tributary of the Çoruh, the Greek Akampsis. The river flows through Sarp, bisecting the village, leaving half of the villagers in Turkey and the other half in what was up until the end of 1991 the U. S. S. R. and is now Georgia. The Akampsis has served as the boundary on this coast since antiquity, as Bryer and Winfield note:

Despite, or because of, the singular peoples who give this stretch its character, the east Pontic border is one of the world's most stable and enduring. For almost two millennia the coastal boundary between Anatolia and the Caucasian powers has found its way back to the mouth of the Akampsis (Çoruh) River after each upheaval. To east and north lay the ancient Laz kingdom, client of Rome from the first century (confirmed in 378), of Persia from 457, and of Byzantium from 522 (confirmed in 561). Yet it is not a cultural boundary, for some Causasian people were caught west of it, the only Georgians to live in Anatolia and retain their identity. Separated from the Laz kingdom, they were perhaps not so much Laz proper as the *autonomoi anthropi* (autonomous people) whom Procopius knew, replacing or descended from the Becheroi, Byzeres, Echecheirieis, and monstrous Mosynoikoi of antiquity. Yet they survived, and survive as "Laz" under successive Byzantine, Trapezuntine, and Turkish rule long after the kingdom of Lazia and its people were forgotten.

Sarp is near the site of ancient Apsaros, where there are the remains of a fortified Roman encampment similar to Canayer at Araklı. The site is impressive in its dimensions, the camp measuring 195 by 242 meters, with the remains of gateways on all four sides. During late Roman and early Byzantine times this fortified camp was the northwesternmost stronghold of the Empire, as it was again in the days of the Grand Comneni.

Apsaros was the legendary burial place of Medea's brother Apsyrtos, whose tomb here was shown to travelers in Classical times. This is a reminder that we are now on the border of the ancient land of Colchis, of which Strabo writes thus in his description of the eastern end of the Euxine:

The great fame that this country had in early times is disclosed in myths, which refer in an obscure way to the expedition of Jason as having proceeded as far as Media....It is said that in their country [Colchis] gold is carried down by the mountain currents, and that the barbarians obtain it by means of perforated troughs and fleecy skins, and that this is the origin of the myth of the golden fleece.

CHAPTER EIGHT

HOPA TO ARTVİN AND YUSUFELİ

Our next itinerary will take us inland from Hopa up into the mountains of northeastern Anatolia, the Pontic Alps. Highway 010 begins its ascent soon after leaving the coast, and eleven kilometers out of Hopa it goes over the Cankurtaran pass at an altitude of 690 meters. Then 25 kilometers farther along it brings us to Borçka, a mountain town at the confluence of the Çoruh Nehri, the Greek River Akampsis, and one of its tributaries, the Murgul Çayı, the ancient Mourgoule.

Borçka, known to the Georgians as Phortchka, has been identified tentatively as the medieval Greek Soterioupolis. The only remnant of the medieval town is a small castle on a rocky eminence above the west bank of the Margoule beside the highway. Within the castle there is a ruined chapel that may possibly be the church of the Theotokos Atheniotissa, which can be translated as the "Mother of God" or "Our Lady of Athens." This church is mentioned in the proceedings of a church synod held in Constantinople in 1364.

Beyond Borçka the highway follows the course of the Çoruh, a torrential river which flows along a savage gorge that slashes its way through the Pontic Alps, most of the way with vertical walls on either side. The road often runs along narrow ledges that have been carved out of the sheer cliff hundreds of meters above the wild rapids below.

Our journey up the Çoruh and its tributaries will take us through the heart of what in medieval times was the Georgian principality of Tao-Klarjeti and Şavşeti. The medieval Georgian and Armenian kingdoms were both created by a noble family known as the Bagratid. The Georgian kingdom had its beginnings in the early ninth century, when Prince Ashot the Great of the Bagratuni, a branch of the Bagratid, migrated with his followers from Armenia and settled in the mountainous region of northeastern Anatolia then known as Tao, establishing his capital at Ardanoutzi, Turkish Ardanuç. Ashot was on friendly terms with both the caliph in Baghdad and the emperor in Byzantium. The caliph appointed Ashot Prince of Kartli-Iberia, the region that was to be the core of the Georgian kingdom, and the emperor Leo V named him Curopalates, a Byzantine title meaning Guardian of the Palace. Ashot I, or the Curopalates, as he is called to distinguish him from the Armenian Ashot the Great, ruled Tao from his capital at Ardanoutzi in the years 813-20. He and his successors, most notably David Magistros, the Great (r. 956-1001), extended their realm in northeastern Anatolia and the Caucasus, their first aquisition being Klarjeti, the region contiguous to Tao on the east. Ashot's rise to power was aided by the efforts of St. Grigol (Gregory) of Hantza (759-861), who is said by his biographer to have proclaimed that "Georgia is reckoned to consist of those spacious lands in which church services are celebrated and all prayers said in the Georgian tongue." Grigol lived to the age of 102 on a diet of dried cabbage, bread, and water; in his time he was the archimandrite, or director, of twelve monasteries in Klarjeti, five of which he founded or restored, while the other seven were built by his disciples. These and other Georgian monasteries of the area are described by Wachtang Djobadze in *Early Georgian Monasteries of Historic Tao, Klarjeti, and Şavşeti* (1992).

The first of the Bagratuni to proclaim himself King of Georgia was Adarnase IV, who in 888 revived the Iberian monarchy that had been moribund for three centuries. The Georgian kingdom expanded considerably under Bagrat IV (r. 975-1014), but this aroused the anger of the Byzantine emperor Basil II, who invaded Georgia in 1021 and annexed Tao and the region to its east. But Bagrat IV (r. 1027-72) came to terms with the Byzantines in the reign of Romanus III Argyrus, who gave him his daughter Helena in marriage. Bagrat IV died in 1072, the year after the battle of Manzikert, in which Romanus III was utterly defeated by the Selçuk sultan Alparslan. After their victory the Selçuks overran most of Asia Minor, with the Armenian kingdom of the Bagratid being

Map II   Artvin Region: Georgian Churches and Monasteries

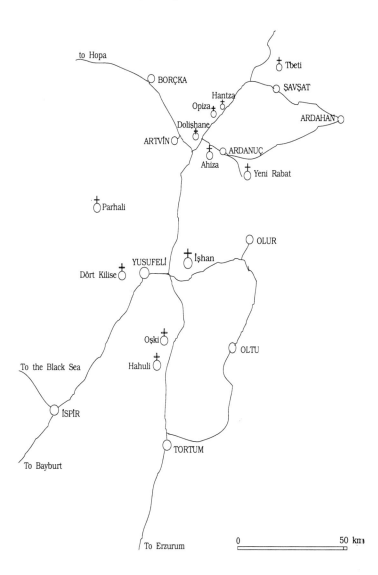

swept away and the Georgian kingdom barely surviving. Georgia revived under David IV (r. 1089-1125), who defeated the Selçuks in 1121 and captured Tblisi the following year, making it his new capital. Before his reign was over he had extended the limits of the Georgian kingdom far beyond its original boundaries, with his realm comprising all of the Caucasus and northeastern Anatolia, including the former dominions of the Armenian kingdom of the Bagratid and its capital at Ani. His great-granddaughter was Queen Thamar, who ruled Georgia in her own right between 1184 and 1213. The Georgian kingdom reached its peak under Queen Thamar; and though it was later overrun in part by various enemies, beginning with the Mongol conquest of eastern Georgia in 1236, it survived until 1804, when it was annexed by Russia, ending one of the longest-lived dynasties in history. The few thousand Georgians who now live in northeastern Turkey continue to speak their native language. All of them are Muslim, their ancestors having converted to Islam in Ottoman times. The churches, monasteries and fortresses erected by their ancestors are among the most interesting buildings in the Pontus, a reminder of the former greatness of the medieval Georgian kingdom. The following description of the Georgians was written by Patriarch Jacques de Vitry around 1225, a time when the Georgian kingdom was in its most flourishing state:

There is also in the East another Christian people, who are very warlike and valiant, being strong in battle and powerful in the number of their warriors. They are much dreaded by the Saracens and have often by their invasions done great damage to the Persians, Medes and Assyrians on whose borders they dwell. They are called Georgians....Whenever they come on pilgrimage to the Lord's Sepulchre, they march into the Holy City with banners displayed, without paying tribute to anyone, for the Saracens dare in no wise molest them. They wear their hair and beards about a cubit long, and have hats upon their heads.

After a drive of 28 kilometers along the Çoruh gorge we come to the turnoff for Artvin, the provincial capital, which is situated five kilometers away from the main highway. The town is built on one of the eastern spurs of the Kaçkar Mountains, with its houses rising on terraces from the Çoruh valley up to the peaks of the hills above, one of which is crowned with the ruins of a medieval fortress built by the Bagratid. The official elevation of Artvin is 500 meters, but that is just a rough average, for parts of it are much higher: its citizens claim that there is no place in the town that is either large enough or level enough to be a football field. Artvin is one of the most progressive towns in Turkey, noted for the excellence of its schools and the high level of its culture, as well as for its bracing climate.

The best time to visit Artvin is the last weekend in June, when the renowned Kavkasör festival is held in an enormous *yayla* high above the town, with the snow-capped peaks of the Kaçkar Mountains rising to the west. The first day of the festival is given over to cultural activities, including recitations of poetry and performances of Georgian folk dances; on the second day there is a wrestling tournament; and on the third day the fête climaxes with the famous bullfighting contest, which usually draws a crowd of some 20,000, the majority of them Georgian-speakers. The contest involves more than a hundred bulls paired off in various classes determined by their girth, each pair confronting one another and eventually locking horns, the struggle ending when one of them gives up and flees, leaving the field to the victor, almost always without injury, for the moment there is a sign of blood the fight is halted. It is an elimination contest that continues until a champion emerges in each class, the highest being the heavyweight, bedecked with wreaths as he is led around the field to the cheers of the crowd, who have spent the afternoon fleeing from the wild charges of defeated bulls running from the victors. While the competition is underway families and groups of friends are celebrating in embowered enclosures they have built on the natural amphitheater of the surrounding hillside, roasting lambs for their feast, to which the visitor is always welcomed, the men dancing the *horon* to the accompaniment of the *kemençe,* the clarinet, and the Turkish bagpipes, enormous quantities of alcohol being consumed in the process. When we last attended the festival we were invited to join one of these feasts, where we were serenaded by a tipsy bagpiper who said he was eighty years old, his white hair and beard still tinged with traces of its original ginger-red, his bright blue eyes sparkling with joy despite the numbing effects of the *rakı* that he downed whenever he paused to catch his breath, then resuming his playing with his head thrust back as if he were piping a medieval Georgian army into battle, looking like a lost survivor from a more heroic age of the Pontus.

After leaving Artvin we return to the highway and continue for eleven kilometers to the turnoff for Şavşat, where we head northeast along the north bank of the Şavşat Suyu, known to the Georgians as the Imerhev River. This takes us into the heart of the region that was once the Georgian principality of Tao-Klarjeti.

Some eight kilometers along highway 101 we turn left for the village of Hamamlı, where we find the former Georgian church known in Turkish as Dolişhane. The building now serves as the village mosque and is therefore relatively well preserved. The church is a cruciform domed structure in which the cross is inscribed within a rectangle, the interior measuring 15.80 meters in length and 11.38 meters in width. Four slightly pointed stepped arches rise from the corners where the arms of the cross intersect to support the dome, the transition from the square to the circular cornice being made by four pendentives. The eastern arm ends in a semicircular apse flanked by two side chambers that open into the side arms. The western arm opens to a rectangular narthex with a choir above that has now almost vanished, along with the western annex. Doors on either side of the narthex led to rectangular chambers that flanked the long western arm of the cross, but only the room on the north side, now half-filled with debris, has survived. The apse and perhaps the dome were decorated with paintings, but those that may have survived in the upper zone of the church are now completely covered with whitewash. The lower half of the apse contains remnants of paintings of the apostles and church fathers inscribed with Georgian letters; these have been dated to the thirteenth century. The crypt preserves life-size paintings of the four evangelists, whose faces have been damaged by vandals.

The conical roof contains only part of its original tiled roof, the remainder having been replaced by cement. The drum that supports the dome is dodecagonal on the exterior, with twelve blind arches resting on twin colonnettes with palmette capitals. The arch of the window in the south arm has on its exterior an inscription recording that the founder is King Sumbat I (r. 954-58), who is shown in a relief in the southeast blind arch of the dome's drum. The window is flanked by reliefs of the Archangels Michael and Gabriel, identified by inscriptions. Below Gabriel's figure there is a star of David inscribed in a circle, an allusion to the claim that the Bagratid dynasty was descended from the biblical king David. Between the window and the figure of Gabriel there is a relief bust within a roundel in the form of a sunburst, with an inscription identifying the figure as that of "the deacon Gabriel," who may have been the architect of the church and also its sculptor. A study of the building

Dolişhane Church

by Wachtang Djobadze indicates that King Sumbat only restored the church, which was actually built a few decades earlier by his older brother Bagrat, who died in 945.

Among the other reliefs and inscriptions the most interesting is on the south façade, where the gnomon of a sundial casts its shadow onto one or another of twelve equidistant radiating segments in the form of leaves. When the scholar Marr visited Dolişhane on 21 August 1904 he found that this sundial was being used to regulate the irrigation of the orchards around the church, and apparently it still serves the same purpose today.

Returning to the highway, we go on for another two kilometers and then turn right for Ardanuç, a drive of eleven kilometers up the north bank of the Ardanuç Suyu, also known as the Bulanık, a tributary of the Şavşat Suyu. After a drive of about five kilometers we see the ruins of a medieval Georgian fortress known as Ferhatlı Kale crowning the peak of a craggy mountain to the south. This was part of the monastery of Ahiza, the fragments of whose ruins lie around the fortress. The monastery is believed to have been built some time between the end of the ninth century and the middle of the tenth.

Ardanuç is situated on a small plateau at the confluence of the Bulanık and two of its tributaries, whose deep ravines surround the town on three sides. Modern Ardanuç is on the plateau, while old Ardanoutzi clusters around a huge table rock that served as the acropolis of the medieval Georgian city. Ardanoutzi was founded in the fifth century by the Georgian king, Wachtang Gorgosal; subsequently it became the capital of the original Georgian principality of Tao-Klarjeti, founded by Ashot I in 813. Through the patronage of Ashot and his successors the strategically located city developed into an important trading center, one of the main links on the commercial route between Constantinople and Trebizond. The emperor Constantine VII Porphyrogenitus, writing in the mid-tenth century in his work on the imperial Byzantine administration, lists it among the most important trade centers in northeastern Asia Minor. He has this to say:

The city of Ardanoutzin is very strongly defended, and has moreover a considerable suburban area like a provincial city, and the commerce of Trapezus [Trebizond] and of Iberia and of Abasgia and from the whole country of Armenia and Syria comes to it, and it has an enormous customs revenue from this commerce.

The ruined walls of medieval Ardanoutzi still ring the great acropolis rock, which today can only be scaled at one point above the old town by means of a ladder, a precarious ascent that adds to the drama of the site. Among the ruins on the acropolis the most significant are those of a small church, which has been dated to the ninth century. Djobadze suggests that this was the private chapel of Ashot I Curopalates, who dedicated it to the Apostles Peter and Paul; after his assassination on 26 January 826 he was buried here. The church is mentioned by the Georgian chronicler Sumbat Davit'isdze, who writes thus of the founding of Ardanoutzi and its fortress by King Ashot:

And [Ashot] was sovereign over Şavşeti and Klarjeti and he found in the forest of Klarjeti a certain rock, where originally Wahtang Gorgasal had built a fortress named Artanuji which had subsequently been destroyed by Qru of Baghdad. Ashot renewed and built it as a fortress and below it he built a city. And inside that castle he built the church of the Holy Apostles Peter and Paul and made his sepulcher in it. And he established himself to reside in that castle.

A road leads southeastward from Ardanuç to the village of Bulanik, a drive of 16 kilometers. From Bulanık a path leads to the Georgian monastery of Yeni Rabat, a walk of about one kilometer.

Like many of the other Georgian churches in the region, Yeni Rabat is a domed cruciform structure, similar in plan and dimensions to Dolişhane. The structure is fairly well preserved. The drum of the dome is articulated by twenty-four blind arches, half of which cover triangular niches. The arches are supported by twin spiral half colonnettes, topped by two joined globes with a square impost above. The twin windows of the east and south arms of the cross are carved with a continuous chain of overlapping half-circles, formed by double-grooved bands, interlaced with an inner and outer ribbon, and framed by a salient fillet and grooved spiral mouldings. The south external face of the west arm is decorated with a tightly woven rosette, formed by tensely intertwined double-grooved bands in concentric circles; to the right of this there is an eight-petalled rosette set in a circle.

Djobadze dates the present church to the latter years of the first half of the eleventh century. He also suggests that this may have been a rebuilding of the monastery of Satberdi, which is known to have been located in his region. Satberdi was founded by St. Grigol of Hantza with the aid of King Ashot the Great and his three sons. Grigol's biographer writes: "And Grigol made the sign of the cross over this eminent place, and the building of the monastery and also of the cells began; and day by day the construction proceeded successfully." The monks of Satberdi were renowned as men of letters and as copiers and illustrators of manuscripts, extant examples of which are in museums in Tbilisi and elsewhere in Georgia.

Returning to highway 101, we now turn right and continue driving northeastward along the Şavşat Suyu. After five kilometers we turn left on a road signposted for Ortaköy, which after some three kilometers brings us within walking distance of the Opiza monastery.

The monastery consists of the church of St. John the Baptist, along with its refectory, storage rooms, and some unidentified facilities. The monastery was founded soon after 750 and rebuilt in the middle of the tenth century by King Ashot IV and his brother David. When St. Grigol of Hantza first arrived in Klarjeti, in 782, he established himself in Opiza for two years, after which he went on to found the famous monastery in Hantza, from which he takes his name.

The church is a cruciform domed building with a very elongated barrel-vaulted western arm divided into five bays by arches. The drum of the dome, circular within and dodecagonal on the exterior, rest on four arches, the spherical angles at the corners formed by

Yeni Rabat Church

architectural elements that have been described as a fusion of pendentives and squinches. The exterior surfaces of the drum has twelve blind arches, six of which have windows; at the corners there are paired colonnettes surmounted by twin Corinthian capitals. The most remarkable feature of the exterior is the roof of the dome, whose top shell is in the form of a Faltendach, or half-opened umbrella, forming twelve connected gables with stepped cornices. The only figural sculpture on the church is now in the National Museum of Arts in Tblisi; this consists of two framed reliefs of King Ashot IV and his brother David flanking the enthroned figure of Christ. Ashot is presenting to Christ the model of a cruciform domed church resembling Opiza, of which he and his brother were the donors.

The monks of Opiza were renowned for their scholarship and also as craftsmen in precious metals, gems, and enamels, outstanding examples of which are preserved in the Tblisi Museum. The two most famous of these craftsmen were the goldsmiths Besken and Beka Opizari, whose works are among the greatest treasures of the museum.

Returning to highway 101, we continue driving toward Şavşat for about another five kilometers before we turn left on a road that goes along the right bank of the Karçhal River, eventually bringing us to the hamlet of Porta. There we see the impressive ruins of a Georgian monastery that has been identified as that of St. George of Hantza. This was the first monastery founded by St. Grigol of Hantza, who was guided here in 782 by the Holy Spirit. The site of the monastery and the way of life of its brethren are well described by St. Grigol's biographer, Giorgi Mercule, a monk of Hantza, who in 951 wrote:

This solitary spot is well balanced by nature, for neither the scorching heat will burn, nor exceeding cold will discomfort man here. Because it is distinct from its neighboring land by being dry, torrid, and exposed to the sun, the soles of a man's feet will never be muddied while walking. The water is pleasant and the wood is plentiful; the sandy soil grows tall, dense forests and from them spring forth tasty free-flowing wells. Thus God has endowed this land with a joyful nature, and it is pathless and inaccessible to those who lead a worldly life, because the dwellings of these monks are located on precipitous and remote crags...surrounded on all sides by mountains, gorges, and waterfalls flowing down from the frightening heights. But there is no pasture to be mown, nor wheat fields to be plowed, and therefore food is brought on the backs of donkeys with great difficulty. Yet there is some wine which has been planted by the brethren with the utmost toil and hardship, and there are also orchards and herbs in the fields and wild pears in abundance, and with all this the hearts of these monks are fearless against the hardships caused by the unbelievers and non-Christians, and in the face of all kinds of troubles from the animosity among the worldly rulers. And in this completely peaceful manner they exist calmly and glorify Christ.

Mercule goes on to write of how St. Grigol built the first church on this site, a wooden structure, after which he erected a dormitory and a refectory to house and feed the monks. Later, probably early in the ninth century, Grigol built a masonry church with funds supplied by the local feudal lord, Gabriel Dapanculi. Less than a century later a new and larger church was erected by Ashot IV Kuhi, king of Klarjeti in the years 909-18, a man who "overwhelmed Hantza with countless donations."

The monastery, which is built on a site leveled off on the southeastern slope of a mountain, was surrounded by a retaining wall measuring more than 53 meters from north to south and 38 meters from east to west, its height ranging from six to eight meters. The wall survives along most of the south and east sides. Aside from the church, the largest surviving structure in the monastery is the refectory, a two-aisled hall on the southeast corner of the mandra, or enclosure. Adjoining this to the north along the eastern retaining wall is the dormitory, with an oratory on the south and adjacent to it three small cells opening onto a balcony. The dormitory originally consisted of three stories, with three rooms on each level; there were apparently additional living quarters on the western side of the enclosure. The cells in the dormitory are very plain, without niches, chimneys or fireplaces, or indeed any form of decoration. This reflects the asceticism of life in the Hantza monastery, an asceticism described in the following passage taken from Giorgi Mercule's biography of St. Grigol:

> ...in those days of our blessed father Grigol, the rules for his disciples were very severe. In their cells were small bedsteads with a minimum of bedding and just one water jug in each. They had no other luxury in eating or drinking apart from what they ate at the common table; this was all they lived on. Many of them did not drink any wine at all, while those who did partook of it in strict moderation. There were no chimneys in their cells because no fires were lit. Nor did they light candles at night. Yet the night was spent in chanting psalms and the day in the constant reading of books and in prayer, as David says: "Yet the Lord will command his loving kindness in the daytime, and in the night his song shall be with me." (Psalms 42: 8).

Beyond the dormitory to the south is the towering monastic church, which stands on a high terrace of the southward-sloping, stepped plateau. In plan the church is a domed cross inscribed in a rectangle, its interior dimensions measuring 10.50 meters in width and 16.85 meters in length, including a semicircular apse flanked by rectangular chambers opening into the side arms. The west arm of the cross is in effect a three-aisled basilica, with the wide central area of the nave separated from the narrow side aisles by two pairs of piers. Four slightly pointed ribbed arches spring from the corners of the central square of the cross to support the drum of the dome, which is octagonal on the interior and dodecagonal on the exterior. Squinches make the transition from the square bay to the octagonal base of the drum. The exterior of the drum is divided into twelve blind arches supported by paired colonnettes surmounted by Doric-type capitals. Apparently the colonnettes were originally painted purple, as evidenced by traces of the pigment that still adheres to them, which seems to have been a not uncommon practice in the church architecture of Tao-Klarjeti. The roof of the dome is divided into twelve equal segments of cusped and furrowed ribbings in the form of a half-opened umbrella. These segments form gables with rectangular cornices on top of the blind arcades. The exterior walls are made of squared and smoothed blocks of stone in even courses, with polychromatic blocks inserted here and there for effect.

The domed structure on the west side of the enclosure is the bell tower. This is in two stories, the lower one one square and the upper, the bell tower itself, sixteen-sided, with round-arched windows in alternate sides. The conical roof is formed by sixteen segments of ribbed interlocking stone tiles ending in zigzag eaves. The bell tower is much later than the church itself, and Djobadze dates it to the fourteenth century.

The Hantza monastery was the one most renowned in the Georgian world for the scholarship of its monks, who wrote, copied, and translated religious and literary works. The most famous of its scholars was Giorgi Mercule, who in addition to his biography of St. Grigol composed a number of hymnographic works. The works of Mercule, written in the mid-tenth century, were widely distributed in Georgia, and it was said of him that "by the rivers of his wisdom were irrigated the monasteries in Klarjeti."

Returning to the highway, we continue along in the same direction. We then finally come to Şavşat, a pretty town of timber houses in a beautiful valley ringed round with towering mountains, several of which are over 3,000 meters high. The town was known in medieval Georgia as Şavşeti, capital of the province of the same name, which in 1008 became part of the kingdom of Tao-Klarjeti. Şavşat is known for its fine kilims, many of which are now made and sold in the People's Education Center (Halk Eğitim Merkezi). The people of Şavşat are also noted for their progressive and enlightened attitude, as evidenced by the town's having two bookshops, a remarkable fact for a remote little Anatolian town.

The only surviving remnant of medieval Şavşeti is the impressive Georgian fortress known as Şavşat Kalesi, which is a short way to the east of town on highway 010. The fortress probably dates from the early eleventh century.

A secondary road that branches off from highway 010 just west of Şavşat is signposted for Veliköy. We continue along this road until the turn-off for Cevizli, which brings us to the monastery of Tbeti, 15 kilometers northwest of Şavşat.

The Georgian chronicler Vahusti writes that "in Tbeti is a well-built and very beautifully adorned domed church built by Ashot Kuhi Bagrationi." This was King Ashot IV, and so the monastery of Tbeti can be dated to the time of his reign, 909-18, though it was rebuilt and enlarged in the eleventh century and renovated in the thirteenth century. The church was in perfect condition until the early 1960s, when it was badly damaged by locals who used it as a quarry for building materials.

The plan of the church is a domed cross, its interior measuring 22.80 meters along the east-west arm, including the semicircular apse at the eastern end, and 22.40 meters along the north-south arm, including the apsidal chapel at the northern end. This chapel had a second story that opened to the main area of the church through three profiled open arches supported by two short columns. The main apse is flanked by two chambers that connect directly with the sanctuary. At the west end of the church, which is now almost destroyed, there was a gallery resting on pilasters on the north and south walls and an elaborate column in the center; this was used as the women's gallery. At the crossing of the two arms four heavy piers, now destroyed, supported the arches that carried the drum and the dome.

The interior of the church was completely covered with paintings except for the south and north arms, which leads one to conclude that these sections were added after the church had been decorated. The paintings in the apse were still intact in 1888, but the destruction of the church in the early 1960s has left only fragments of these in place. On the north wall of the west arm there was a monolithic three-dimensional sculpture of King Ashot IV, who was shown holding a model of the church. The sculpture is now in the Tbilisi

Şavşat Kalesi

Museum, though part of the King's face has been hacked off and other parts of the sculpture are missing, including most of the church model.

The monastery of Tbeti was a center of culture, and a number of its monks were renowned scholars, scribes and hymnographers. These included the hagiographer Step'ane Mtbevari (of Tbeti), the translator David Tbeli, the scribe Akvila Mtbevari and the hymnist Ioane Mtbevari, some of whose works are preserved in Georgia and Russia.

We now return to the crossroads southeast of Artvin, where we head southward on highway 950. At Zeytinlik we cross the Çoruh, after which we drive along the west bank of the river through a tremendous gorge, whose almost vertical cliffs drop sheer into the wild river below.

Some 50 kilometers beyond the Şavşat intersection we turn off on the right for Yusufeli, a drive of ten kilometers Here we continue along the Çoruh to its confluence with the Barhal Çayı, another tempestuous river, whose sources are up among the highest peaks in the Kaçkar range.

Yusufeli stands astride the Barhal Çayı a short way upstream from the Çoruh, with the river roaring right through the center of town, spanned by two swaying bridges. It is a very lively town, almost wild west in its atmosphere, its most popular night spot a beer hall suspended on corbels above the boiling rapids of the Barhal Çayı, most of its habitués being burly mountaineers from the isolated hamlets of the surrounding mountains. There is absolutely nothing to see in Yusufeli other than the river; but it is a perfect base for exploring the surrounding region, which in the medieval era formed the southwestern corner of Tao-Klarjeti.

Our initial excursion from Yusufeli will first take us back to the turnoff from highway 950, which is at the confluence of the Çoruh and the Oltu Çayı. From there we drive eastward for eight kilometers to the confluence of the Oltu and the Tortum Çayı. There we leave highway 950 and continue eastward along highway 060, which goes along the north bank of the Oltu. About six kilometers from the crossroads we turn left for İşhan, a little mountain village approached by a vertiginous road that winds up from the valley of the Oltu in an endless series of bends with ever-expanding views of the surrounding landscape. After coming to the village we follow the main street directly to the great cathedral of İşhan, one of the most impressive of the surviving Georgian churches in the region.

The history of İşhan as a Georgian religious center goes back to the mid-seventh century, when Nerses III, the Catholicos of Armenia, sought refuge here to escape persecution for his support of the creed published at the Council of Chalcedon in 451. Nerses built a tetraconch church in İşhan, part of which is still in existence. This church seems to have been destroyed during an Arab raid in the years 736-38. The building remain in ruins until the third decade of the ninth century, when St. Grigol of Hantza and his cousin Saba were led to the site by divine guidance. Giorgi Mercule tells the story in his biography of Grigol:

Grigol and Saba reached the vicinity of Ishan, and God revealed to them the original greatness of this site and announced to them that Işhan would be restored again by the hand of Saba. And the trail to get there was shown to them, for at that time this place was inaccessible to man. When they arrived in Işhan they were very happy to find this glorious place, because it provided both carnal and spiritual consolation.

Mercule goes on to write of how Grigol and Saba went back to Hantza to seek help from their brethren. This done, Saba then set out on his return journey to İşhan. Mercule describes it thus:

...after several days Grigol assigned to Saba two disciples from the monastery of Hantza and sent them to Işhan, while he himself remained in Hantza to direct the spiritual life of the monastery in accordance with the will of the Lord....By the will of God, Saba became bishop in Ishan—of the Catholic church built originally by the blessed Nerses—and of his throne which for many years had been widowed. Now again took place the spiritual wedding of the cathedral which was built a second time by our blessed Saba with the material support of those God-imbued kings.

The kings referred to by Mercule would have been Ashot the Great and his successors, eight of whom are mentioned in inscriptions in the church. The latest in date of these kings is Bagrat IV (r. 1027-32), who in one inscription is credited with rebuilding the church in 1032, his master mason being Iovane Morçaisdze.

The church is a cruciform domed structure. The total exterior length of the church along the east-west axis is 36.60 meters, while the interior width at the crossing is 19.00 meters. The eastern arm ends in a semicircular apse flanked by two pairs of side chambers. The apse is surrounded by an ambulatory from which it is separated by an exedra, formed by an arcade of eight columns standing on a semircular wall that extends out to the two eastern piers. This is the only part of the original church of Nerses that survives in the present structure. The upper zone of the apse has on either side twin windows opening into the easternmost side chambers, with the arched apertures separated by a single column.

The west arm of the cross consists of two bays 15.15 meters long and 8.95 meters wide, flanked by pilasters on either side. The main entrance to the cathedral was at the western end, and there was another portal on the south side of the westernmost bay. Beyond the northern side of the west arm there is a room 16.10 meters long and 4.80 meters wide in four bays, accessible through a single door near its northeast end.

At the crossing, the dome is supported by four freestanding columns with elaborately decorated bases and capitals. The transition from the square bay to the circular base of the drum is achieved by fluted pendentives surmounted by relieving arches with cable moldings.

The interior of the church was decorated with wall paintings done shortly after the cathedral was rebuilt in 1032. The best-preserved paintings are those in the dome, which is completely covered with a representation of the elevation of the Host, in which the sacred wafer is held aloft by four hovering angels. Below this there are four apocalyptic chariots representing the vision of Zechariah (Zechariah 6:1-15). On the north side a female figure is shown sitting on a bull, the zodiacal sign of the moon.

The outer surfaces of the church are accentuated by quadruple blind arches and stepped composite pilasters, the fronts of which consists of three closely spaced engaged colonnettes, with compound semicircular relieving arches spring from their imposts. The east and south façades are decorated by large crosses set prominently in the central blind arches. The most common of these in Georgian churches of this period is the so-called "leaved cross," characterized by flaring crossarms and with leaves extending upward from the base. The sculptured decoration of the window frames consists almost entirely of interlacing patterns along with geometric and stylized plant motifs. The sole exception is the third window from the west on the south façade of the west arm, which has below it a relief representing a lion and dragon in combat. The latter relief

İşhan Church

İşhan Church, Carving over Main Door

stems from an ancient myth concerning solar eclipses, in which the sun, symbolized by the lion, is swallowed up by a great serpent.

The exterior of the main door to the church is decorated with complex geometrical carvings, of which Djobadze writes that "our portal with its well-balanced and superbly-worked decorative system may be considered one of the outstanding examples of Georgian architecture." The monolithic tympanum of the door contains a lengthy inscription consisting of twelve semicircular lines, of which the first and outer one is carved in much larger characters than the others. The inscription refers to a renovation of the now-vanished south porch during the reign of King Giorgi I (r. 1014-27) by the bishop of İşhan, who refers to himself as the "miserable Antoni."

The exterior surfaces of the drum are accentuated by sixteen blind arches resting on twin spiral colonnettes. Each of the main arches is carved with a variety of interlacing geometrical and plant motifs. Alternate blind arches are pierced by tall, round-arched windows, with those between having tiny circular apertures. The circular frames of the small apertures and the brows of the arched windows are decorated with intricate carvings. The surface between the blind arches and the upper cornice of the drum has a monumental pearl molding on a pearl background. The upper cornice has a projecting molding in a kind of herringbone pattern, surmounted by a cable molding with scallops above. The conical dome was originally covered with polychromatic glazed pan-and-role tiles; these have now completely vanished, but the alternating purple and green stripes of the roofing remain.

Some thirty meters south of the cathedral there is a beautiful chapel, the dedicatory inscription of which tells us that it was erected in 1006 by Gurgen, who was known in his time as the King of Kings. (An earlier Gurgen was known as the Duke of Dukes.) The chapel is a single-nave structure of two bays divided by an arch and a pair of supporting pilasters. It has windows in both the apse and the west end, and the doorway is on the north side of the western bay. The frames of the door and both of the windows are lavishly decorated with intricate carvings. The most interesting of the sculptured decorations is on the omega-shaped brow of the tympanum of the doorway. This consists of twenty intertwined squares, all but one of them depicting birds and animals both real and mythological. The center square depicts a bunch of grapes. The relief is thought to represent the garden of Eden, to which the door of the chapel is the symbolic entrance, as evidenced by the accompanying inscription, which states that "this is the gate of the Lord into which the righteous shall enter."

Returning to the crossroads at the confluence of the Oltu and the Tortum, we now turn south along highway 959. This brings us to the gorge of the Tortum, which is just as wild as those of Çoruh and the Barhal. Hamilton came down this gorge in his approach to Tortum on his journey through Asia Minor in 1836-37, his description giving us a vivid picture of the difficulties of travelling in this wild and inaccessible region then, before the first roads were laid down through these canyons:

I had been led to expect a wild and difficult pass today through the mountain glens, but I was not prepared for the tremendous but beautiful scenery which awaited me after proceeding about two miles in this northern direction. After receiving the waters of two or three tributary streams, the valley suddenly contracted, and the raging torrent, hemmed in between perpendicular cliffs nearly a thousand feet in height, urged its way through a deep and gloomy den, in many places without leaving the smallest space of ground on either side, whereon to make a road. Sometimes a slippery and dangerous path had been made along the talu of the debris which had fallen from the lofty cliffs; but this, as well as the talu itself, had in many places been washed away by the violence of the torrent; and for a mile and a half we were constantly obliged to descend into the bed of the stream, and pick our way as well we could, amidst the huge stones with which it was encumbered....Emerging from this stupendous pass, we crossed a muddy stream flowing from the east, with which the principal river for some distance refuses to mingle its pure and limpid waters. Leaving the bed of the river, we encountered a mass of dark volcanic rock, which for nearly two miles further formed a succession of narrow passes, through which the river had forced a deep and tortuous passage far below the road, along which we were leading our fatigued and frightened horses....

Just beyond a turnoff for the village of Çağlayan we pass on our left Tortum Şelalesi, the waterfall at the northern outlet of Tortum Gölü, a long and narrow lake whose turquoise waters are surrounded by emerald green mountains. At the southern end of the lake there is a turnoff on the right for the village of Çamlıyamaç, where we find the great monastic church of Oşki, or Ösk Vank.

The monastery of Öşki, whose church was dedicated to St. John the Baptist, was also an important administrative center for the rulers of Tao-Klarjeti. As is the case elsewhere in this region, virtually nothing remains of the secular structures. All that survives of Oşki are the church itself and the remains of a few monastic buildings, which have been identified as the refectory, the seminary, the scriptorium, and the residence of the bishop, along with two chapels and other ruins. Most of the church is fairly well preserved, though its barrel vaults have completely disappeared and most of the pilaster blocks have been removed. Nevertheless it is still the most impressive of all the Georgian churches in the region.

Inscriptions record that the church was built by two sons of Adarnase III, who died in 963; they were David III Magistros, and Bagrat, Duke of Dukes. This, together with other documentary evidence, reveals that the church was built in the years 963-73. The only part of the original church that has been transformed is the dome, which was given a new roof by the Byzantine emperor Basil II and his successor Constantine VIII sometime between 1022 and 1025. In 1036 the interior walls of the church were decorated with paintings by Jojik Patrikios, a Georgian nobleman.

The church is cruciform in plan, with each of the east, north and south arms terminating in a semicircular apse flanked by apsidal side chambers. The west arm consists of a long barrel-vaulted nave, beyond which there was an annex, now vanished. The interior length of the church without its west annex is 40.60 meters; its maximum width is 27 meters and its greatest height is 34 meters. All three of the apses are pierced with three windows. The side chambers flanking the main eastern apse are two storys high and have a single window in the apse. These chambers connect directly to the sanctuary, whereas in all of the other churches of the region they open into the main area of the building.

The north and south crossarms are identical. They differ from the eastern apse only in their dimensions, their apses being slightly wider but shallower. Two of the church's four doors are located in these apses. The side chambers flanking these apses are two-storied.

The elongated western arm is 19.40 meters in length and 9.70 meters in width. Engaged piers on either side divide it into five bays of different length. On the north side of the west arm there is a two-storied gallery, accessible from the northwest of the west crossarm. The lower gallery is barrel-vaulted and ends on the east side in a semicircular apse. The upper gallery may have been accessible by a wooden staircase from the west; it appears that this was the gynaceum, or women's section.

A door midway along the south side of the western arm leads to a porch extending along the southwestern wall of the church. The porch, which is 15.50 meters long and 2.55 meters wide, consists of four bays, and at its eastern end is a semicircular apse decorated with paintings. All four of the bays are surmounted by shallow scalloped domes adorned with intricate designs charaterized by geometrical interlacery and plant motifs, each one different from the others. The south side of the porch rests on four columns, all of them different from one another in form and decoration, the westernmost one, which is octagonal, having an appreciably larger girth than the others. Four piers to the west of these columns support a barrel-vaulted outer porch, 14.50 meters long and 1.25 meters wide, with a narrow apsidal niche at its eastern end. The broken cornice of this porch is accentuated by a receding molding and a pearl stringcourse. On the east wall of the outer porch there is a carving of a cross with flared arms, with two pairs of trilobed leaves issuing from its lower arm, symbolic of the tree of life.

Oşki Church

The octagonal western column of the inner colonnade is adorned with floral and figural reliefs, which cover both the shaft and its capital. The shaft is decorated with symmetrically paired interlocking palmettes which almost cover its whole surface. Within it there are fifteen small disembodied human heads, eight of them wearing crowns, and in addition there are several figures, including one, on the west side of the column, of a bearded man kneeling in an attitude of supplication. An accompanying inscription, now almost completely effaced, identifies him as "Grigol, supervisor of the construction," who is also mentioned in another inscription elsewhere in the church. Directly above Grigol's head there is a "deesis" composition, with the figures of the Virgin and St. John the Baptist flanking Christ. On the northwest and southwest sides there are half-figures of the two Syrian physician saints, SS. Cosmas and Damian, the head of the former now preserved in the Tbilisi Museum. The capital is completely covered with reliefs of the whole heavenly hierarchy, including angels, archangels, seraphim,

Oşki Church, Reliefs on South Wall of Crossarm

cherubim, tetramorphs and powers. On the west side above the capital there is a half-figure of St. Simeon the Younger, the famous stylite, or pillar-sitter, of Antioch. On the northwest side above the same capital is the half-figure of St. Nina, who converted the Georgians to Christianity.

The dome and its drum are supported by four massive freestanding piers. The two eastern piers are dodecagonal in plan, while the eastern pair are cruciform and strengthened by four supportive bands. All of the pier bases are circular, their height being about two meters for the eastern pair and three meters for the western. The bases are adorned with moldings and intricate carvings with geometric and floral designs, the decorations being particularly sumptuous on the two western piers. On the east side of each of the western piers there is an elaborate niche with its upper inner surface carved in the form of a cockleshell. On both faces of the southwestern niche there are half-figure reliefs of the two founders of the church; on the left is David III, Magistros, and on the right Bagrat, Duke of Dukes, their features almost completely effaced by vandals. An inscription to the right of David's figure is a supplication addressed to the Virgin, and on the right is one to St. John the Baptist. Just below the conch in the niche are the remains of a painting of Christ, which together with the flanking inscriptions forms an unusual "deesis," a representation that shows Christ between the Virgin Mary and St. John the Baptist.

The four piers are joined by the four slightly pointed, ribbed arches that support the drum of the dome, which has a diameter of 8.95 meters. The transition from the square bay to the circular cornice of the drum is made by four monolithic pendentives, three of which are decorated with tripartite fluting, while the one on the southwest has nine flutings.

There are double-stepped blind arcades on all of the exterior walls of the church except for the west arm. The arches are supported by three-quarter engaged columns. There are five on each side, gradually increasing in size to the dominant central arch; the latter accentuated by a tall window whose frame and brow are decorated with geometric interlacery, with various sculptures above. The central arch in each of the three crossarms is flanked by a pair of triangular scalloped niches.

The south crossarm has a square open porch, its interior being a square 2.85 meters on a side. On the exterior it has a pitched roof with stepped scalloped courses. The interior is covered by a hemispherical saucer dome of three gradually narrowing courses, the last one formed by eight segmental blocks with a circular keystone, alternate stones painted in red to form a cross. The piers and engaged columns of the porch are decorated with carved, floral motifs.

The dome is supported by a twenty-four-sided drum, each side articulated with a blind arch springing from richly-decorated twin colonnettes at the corners. Their bases are accentuated by astragal moldings and paired globes, while the capitals are richly decorated with geometrical and floral motifs and animals, as well as a caryatid. Alternate sides are pierced by round-arched windows, each of which is surmounted by a purple, painted cross decorated with eight-petalled flowers and adorned with precious stones. The upper cornice of the drum has a cable-and-scallop molding, while the lower one has on its south, southeast and north sides large circles painted in red with a carved pearl molding. The north-to-northwest stretch of this cornice has, in place of the pearl molding, carved figures of rabbits placed face to face and a lion chasing an antelope, as well as real and mythological animals within scrolls. The dome is covered by a conical roof of pan-and-roll tiles. These tiles are glazed in dark red, green, and brown.

Above the brow of the middle window in the main apse there is a damaged torso of a lion in relief. On the south wall of the east crossarm five life-size figures are shown in relief, each of them carved out of a limestone monolith. Christ is in the center flanked by the Virgin (now missing) and St. John the Baptist, forming a "deesis," with the figures of donors on the sides, crowned and robed figures each presenting a model of the church. An inscription on the west jamb of the door leading to the south crossarm identifies the donors; the figure on the left is David Magistros, while the one on the right is Bagrat, Duke of Dukes.

The south crossarm is more lavishly decorated with reliefs than any other part of the church. The small second-story window on the east side of the south crossarm is decorated with two monolithic figural reliefs. Above the window there is a hunting scene, while below two lions attack a stag while another lion looks on. Above the sculptured brow of the window in the central blind arcade there is a high relief of an eagle clutching a bull in its talons. The uppermost part of the blind arch is occupied by the relief figures of two angels, with inscriptions identifying the one on the left as the Archangel Michael and the one on the right as the Archangel Gabriel.

The north façade is not as sumptuously decorated as the south. The window under the central blind arch is flanked by reliefs of animals placed face to face, with a lion attacking on the right and on the left a retreating bull.

The west façade is pierced by twin windows, which are flanked by paired spiral columns. The capitals of the outer columns are formed by scooped acanthus leaves emerging from the corners, while the mullion is emphasized by a fluted colonnette, its capital decorated with grape clusters suspended below the abacus. The monolithic arches of the windows are decorated with a composition in which a lion is attacking a bull on the left. On the right there is a pair of griffins placed face to face, to the left of which there is another fabulous beast known as the senmurw.

Above the center of the twin windows there is a relief showing the half figure of St. Simeon the Younger, who is on a tripartite stepped base representing the pillar on which he perched outside his monastery in Antioch. The entire composition is surrounded by a large arch decorated with interlacing patterns, fillets, and a roundel decorated with a spiral.

We continue driving south along highway 950, passing on our left the village of Uzundere, and then nine kilometers farther along we turn right on a rough track that leads along a valley of orchards

for seven kilometers. This brings us to the village of Bağlarbaşı
Köyü, where we find the Georgian monastery of Hahuli.

A wall three meters high encloses the monastery complex, which
includes the main church, four chapels and a gateway, as well as
the barely recognizable foundations of other buildings, including
refectories, dwelling places for the monks, a library-scriptorium,
workshops, etc. Two of the chapels are badly damaged, but the
main church is remarkably well preserved, owing to its being used
as the village mosque. The church dates from the second half of the
tenth century and is another foundation of David Magistros; it was
originally dedicated to the All-Holy Mother of God.

The church is a cruciform domed structure; its maximum interior
length is 34.43 meters; and its greatest width is 24.00 meters. Its
eastern arm ends in a semicircular apse flanked by a pair of apsidal
chambers opening into the main area of the church. There are two
rectangular niches on the north and south walls of the presbytery,
and around the periphery of the apse there are nine arched niches
that rise to a height of about five meters.

The almost square west arm is in plan a three-aisled basilica,
whose central aisle is three times the width of those on the sides,
from which it is separated by round-arched arcades formed by
three pairs of piers, of which the eastern ones support the western
side of the dome. Each of the eastern piers has a niche three meters
high framed by cable twist strips, its round-arched top surmounted
by interltwined geometric crosses. Both niches were covered with
paintings, of which some fragments remain in the upper part of the
northern one.

The dome over the crossing rests on the western terminations of
the apse walls and on the piers at the east ends of the west arms.
The transition from the square bay to the circular base of the dome's
drum is made by fluted pendentives, flanked by tiny half domes.

The interior walls of the church are revetted with smoothly
finished blocks. Towards the end of the eleventh century the walls
and other interior surfaces were decorated with paintings, fragments
of which can still be seen. Among these is a fragment of a painting

Huhuli Church

on the dome depicting the ascension of Elias, a very rare theme.

The only sculptural decoration on the east façade is above the apse window. It consists of a monolithic arch decorated with fillet and astragal moldings. Directly over the window there is a fillet covered by leaves stemming from two vases. The space between the arch of the window and the outer arch of the brow is filled with thirteen radial segments, composed of alternating yellowish limestone blocks and purplish bricks. The large semicircular brow is decorated with cable moldings, interlacing circles and a floral motif of continuous paired leaves.

The only decoration on the west façade is above the window of the west arm. This is similar to that of the east window, with some modifications, such as a simpler molding on its keystone, and with the number of radiating yellow and purple segments increasing to seventeen. The window brow is decorated with stylized split palmettes.

The north façades of the church are almost completely devoid of sculptural decoration. The sculptural decoration of the south façade is concentrated in two locations: around the twin window of the south crossarm and on the south portal.

The twin window of the south crossarm is flanked by paired spiral colonnettes with elaborate bases and capitals unique in Georgian architecture, while the mullion consists of a single Doric shaft. The molding above the twin window is decorated with a stylized heart pattern. Above the center of the twin windows there is a huge eagle with outspread wings, carved almost in the round.

The south portal is one of the most outstanding features of the church, particularly because of the interesting sculptures around it. The door and its tympanum are framed by interlacing patterns. The tympanum contains a relief representing the exaltation of the Cross, which is held by four angels. On either side of the door there are reliefs of human and animal figures, including fabulous creatures, though the sculptures are now partly covered by the masonry of a porch added in the fourteenth century. The uppermost relief to the left of the door shows the celestial journey of Alexander the Great, whose chariot is being pulled by two griffins; below this is a crouching griffin in a harness; and on the bottom is a lion devouring a bull. On the right at the top is St. Peter, represented as the guardian of the church door, holding a lock and a key; below him is Jonah being disgorged by the whale; below that is a cock with an ornate collar; and on the bottom is a guardian lion.

The exterior of the drum is divided into sixteen sides by a blind arcade, with alternate faces pierced by windows. The windows are surmounted by richly carved semicircular arches with wide purple brows above them. The arches spring from twin spiral colonnettes with rectangular plinths decorated with carvings in geometrical motifs. The capitals are lavishly carved with floral and geometric motifs, with one on the south representing an eagle holding a bull in its talons.

Attached to the south side of the west arm is a barrel-vaulted porch, measuring 11.30 by 4.25 meters, a later addition to the church. Its south side opens into three arches carried by short cruciform piers, flanked by a blind arch on either side. In the southeast corner of the porch a niche contains a crudely carved relief of the Virgin and Christ-child.

There is another annex on the north side of the west arm, a longitudinal barrel-vaulted hall in five bays, measuring 11.50 by 4.20 meters. This was evidently a storage area, as evidenced by the wine jars sunk below the basement.

There is still another annex on the west, measuring 14.00 by 7.85 meters, containing three pairs of bays supported internally by two pillars. Its roof reaches only halfway up the façade of the church, but its floor is much lower. The only entrance is from the west arm, but this is now locked.

The largest of the two surviving chapels is some five meters north of the main church. The other chapel is some five meters to the south of the church. In addition to these there are two other chapels outside the enclosure wall. One of these is about 100 meters to the southeast of the monastery, and the other is perched on a cliff two kilometers to the west.

Hahuli, one of the most prominent cultural centers in Georgia, was used as a monastery until the middle of the sixteenth century. The most famous of its treasure is the Hahuli triptych, a monumental icon of the Virgin now preserved in the Tbilisi Museum.

We now return to Yusufeli to begin a second excursion, which takes us northward on road 08-52 for 40 kilometers up the valley of the Barhal Çayı. This brings us to the monastery of Parhali. All that survives of the monastery is its almost perfectly preserved church, which now serves as a mosque for the village of Barhal. Inscriptions record that this is yet another foundation by David Magistros, built in the years 961-73.

The church is a three-aisled basilica erected on a two-stepped base, its interior measuring 28.40 meters in length and 18.65 meters in width, its height about 22 meters. It originally had four entrances, but now only the portal on the west side is open. The south door has been walled in to create a *mihrap* for the mosque. The nave, which is almost twice the width of the aisles and projects above them, is divided into five bays by four pairs of massive cruciform piers, which support both the longitudinal arches of the aisle arcades and the transverse arches of the three aisles. The third pair of piers from the west end have arched niches on their east side. The pilasters and arch of each of the niches are decorated with floral and figural reliefs, with one of the capitals of the southern niche showing the half figure of an angel in prayer. At the west end of the church there is a gallery supported on two pairs of narrow rectangular piers. The central aisle ends at the east in a semicircular nave, flanked by two pairs of interconnected rectangular chambers, the outer ones opening into the side aisles.

The north and south façades are emphasized by ten stepped blind arches on two levels, the lower one along the side aisles and the upper one along the top half of the nave; the former spring from pilasters and the latter from engaged paired colonnettes.

The east and west façades each have seven blind arches gradually increasing in height toward the center, the two outer ones on either sides under the sloping roofs of the side aisles and the central three under the pitched roof of the nave.

The sculptural decoration of the exterior walls is almost entirely confined to the monolithic arches and brows of the windows. The sculptures fall into two groups according to their style and subject matter. The first and largest group belongs to the east and south façades and to the middle and south parts of the west façade. It is characterized by a variety of stylized motifs, such as half palmettes with lozenges, an interlacing twist, floral elements, and geometrical patterns forming interlaced crosses. The second group consists of animal, bird, and human representations, sometimes in connection with stylized floral motifs. This group is confined to the west part of the north façade, the north portion of the west façade, and to the arches of the lower windows of the north arcade.

Our final excursion from Yusufeli will take us southwestward along highway 98-50 towards İspir. After passing a ruined Georgian fortress on a hilltop site we come to the hamlet of Tekkale, where we turn right on a rough track that leads toward the Georgian church complex of Othta Eklesia, known in Turkish as Dört Kilise, which in both languages means "The Four Churches." Depending on the condition of the road, the final stretch of the approach may be done on foot, a delightful hike up the heavily wooded gorge of a mountain stream. En route one will encounter some of the local people who dwell in the mountains above and who trek down to Yusufeli with loads of timber on their backs, selling it to buy food and other supplies. The women and children are often dressed in the colorful local costumes that have vanished in most other parts of Turkey except among the Yürük and the Kurdish tribes, preserving with it a way of life that one now sees only in the memorabilia of Turkey's ethnographical museums.

Dört Kilise is in a magnificent, isolated site, standing on a spur of the Kaçkar Mountains looking out across the Tortum valley, with absolutely nothing of the modern world in sight to spoil the view, and not a sound other than the soughing of the wind through the surrounding trees. The monastery is surrounded by old orchards of pear, quince, plum, cornelian cherry, mulberry, and walnut trees. Dört Kilise consists of the great basilica, a two-storied mortuary chapel on its southeast, a refectory to its west, and on the northwest side a two-naved hall that has been identified as a seminary and scriptorium. Some 150 meters west of the monastery there are the remains of a small chapel and a two-storied barrel-vaulted building which seems to have served as a dwelling place for the monks. Inscriptions record that here again the founder was David Magistros, who appears to have erected the church in the years 961-65, and to have augmented it some time in the period 978-1001, the latter year being the one in which he died.

The basilica is built to exactly the same plan as the church at Parhali. Its dimensions are almost exactly the same as the Parhali church, its exterior length measuring 28.46 meters, its width 22.07 meters, and its height 22.07 meters. It is quite well preserved except for the north and south exterior walls, which have been used as a quarry by the locals. The exterior walls are articulated throughout by vaulted or blind arcades, the arches of the side aisles resting on double stepped pilasters and those of the nave, projecting above, on

Dört Kilise

paired colonnettes. The most prominent exterior decoration appears on the east façade just under the gable ridge, where there is a blue maltese cross on a round purple background. Below this is an inscription mentioning the founder of the church, David Magistros, who is here referred to as Curopalates, a title he acquired in 978.

The plan of the interior is exactly the same as that of the church of Parhali, a three-aisled basilica with the central nave separated from the side aisles by five pairs of piers, ending at the east in a semicircular apse. The west sides of the easternmost piers have large gabled niches richly framed with paired gable moldings, with smaller arched niches below. The niches were apparently designed to hold large icons. The west end of the nave has a triple-arched gallery resting on two pairs of narrow rectangular piers.

The entire apse below the vault is decorated with paintings separated into five registers by ornamental strips. On the first strip, just below the conch, the enthroned Christ is represented in a mandorla; below is a throne in a medallion supported by two angels, with a cross surmounted by a dove rising from it. In the third register, just above the window in the apse, is the enthroned Virgin flanked by two angels. On either side of the window are two registers, the higher one of which has four prophets on one side and four bishops on the other. Both groups are facing the window. The entire surface of the window soffit is occupied by the upper part of a female figure on a blue background, within a circular frame of lilylike flowers, holding in her right hand a model of the church. An inscription allowed Djobadze to identify the figure as a personification of Zion, or celestial Jerusalem. Djobadze dates the paintings to the period 961-65, when David Magistros first built the church.

The western porch of the church, now in ruins, was a barrel-vaulted structure of three bays. The western part of the porch abuts a longitudinal hall divided into four bays by single arches, a structure that may have been the seminary. Immediately to the north of this is a large structure of interior dimensions 13.00 by 20.80 meters, which has been identified as the refectory. This is divided into two uneven barrel-vaulted naves by a colonnade of four cruciform piers.

Some 6.5 meters southeast of the basilica, at the eastern border of the terrace, there is a two-storied mortuary chapel. The chapel consists of a barrel-vaulted nave inscribed in a rectangle, with a single pair of pilasters and a ribbed arch dividing the hall into two bays. At its east end there is a semicircular apse with a single tier synthronon, a structure that contains a bishop's throne and seats for the clergy. On both sides one finds very narrow compartments opening toward the west.

Dört Kilise is the last of the Georgian monasteries that we will visit on our itinerary, though for those with more time to spare there are a number of other churches and fortresses from the Bagratid period still to be seen in Artvin province. These and the churches we have seen are evocative of the splendours of Georgian civilization in its days of glory. These glories were celebrated in the works of the Georgian poet Shota Rustaveli, who flourished in the mid-thirteenth century. His greatest work is the epic *Vephistqaosani* ("The Knight in the Panther's Skin,"), which David Lang calls "the swan song of Georgia's golden age." During the poets's own lifetime Georgia was overrun by the Mongols, one of a series of invasions that would eventually destroy the civilization that produced the splendid monuments we have seen on this itinerary. Rusteveli's epic ends in the following lament, one in which he mourns the passing of the heroes of Georgia's golden age:

> Their tale is ended like a dream of night. They are passed away, gone beyond the world. Behold the treachery of time: to him who thinks it is long, even for him it is a moment....This is such a world as is not to be trusted by any; it is a moment in the eyes of men, and only long enough for the blinking of the eyelashes. What is the use of searching and striving? Fate will put us to shame. Happy at last is he whom destiny escorts beyond this life into the hereafter!

CHAPTER NINE
YUSUFELİ TO TRABZON VIA THE ZİGANA PASS

Our last itinerary will take us from Yusufeli to İspir and then in turn to Bayburt and Torul, after which we will cross the Zigana Pass and go down via Maçka to Trabzon, thus completing our tour of the Black Sea coast.

The first part of our itinerary will take us from Yusufeli to İspir along highway 08-50, a drive of 79 kilometers. This takes us along the valley of the Çoruh, with the Kaçkar Mountains to our right and to our left the range known as the Mescit Dağları, so that we pass a succession of peaks on both sides of the road, many of them rising to well over 3,000 meters, with the Çoruh torrent roaring away in its canyon below.

Finally we come to İspir, an ancient mountain stronghold on the Çoruh, its tiered houses clustering around the craggy spire of the acropolis rock that dominates the town, crowned by the impressive ruins of the medieval citadel perched high above the river. The scenery is much the same as it was when Hamilton passed this way in 1836, although from the description that follows it would appear that the town has grown considerably in the interim:

...As we advanced, cultivation and vegetation rapidly increased; the hills were covered with wild flowers, amongst which lupins of all colours were conspicuous; and the air was perfumed with the sweet fragrance of the flower of the jujube-tree.

At quarter after four we came in sight of the picturesque castle of Ispir, situated on a rocky point in the middle of the valley, which is here much contracted. The castle commands the narrow pass by which the Tchoruk Su enters the mountains; and at its foot are a few flat-roofed underground houses, adorned with a mosque, honoured by the residence of a Waiwoda [provincial governor], and dignified with the vague name of Cassaba, or town.

The name İspir is derived from the ancient Greek name Syspiritis, the earliest reference to which is in Strabo's *Geography*. Strabo refers to this town in connection with the hero Armenus the Thessalian, who in one version of the myth accompanies Jason on his voyage aboard the *Argo* in quest of the golden fleece. According to Strabo, Armenus and his followers parted company with Jason and the other Argonauts in Colchis; and from there they traveled back to eastern Asia Minor, where some of them settled in Syspiritis and others in a town on the Euphrates called Adiabene. Strabo then goes on to say that Armenus "left Armenia named after himself," a little-known legend that seems to have eluded all travelers to this seldom-visited region of eastern Anatolia.

When the Persians captured Syspiritis early in Justinian's reign they called it Pharangion, but after the town was retaken by Belisarius it reverted to its original name. İspir was for centuries a frontier town, taken in turn by the Persians, Byzantines, Selçuks, the Grand Comneni of Trebizond, the Bagratid kings of Georgia, and various Türkmen tribes, until it finally became a permanent part of the Ottoman Empire when Selim I captured it on his Persian campaign in 1516. At that time, though it had been in Turkish hands for most of the previous three centuries, İspir was a predominantly Christian town, mostly Armenian; and in the Ottoman census of 1530 only three percent of the population was Muslim.

The citadel and the other principal monuments of İspir are apparently all works of the famous Melik Mugisettin Tuğrul Şah, who held the town in the first quarter of the twelfth century. These monuments include the citadel and the fortification walls of İspir, which were apparently erected originally in the medieval Byzantine period and then rebuilt by Melik, as well as two mosques: Sultan Melik Mescidi on the acropolis, and the Tuğrulşah Camii in the lower town. Sultan Melik Mescidi is one of two prominent monuments on the acropolis, the other being a ruined church that somewhat surpasses the mosque in size. It was long thought that this church was founded by the Grand Comneni of Trebizond, on one of the occasions when they recaptured the town from the Turks.

İspir, View of the Acropolis with Byzantine Church and Selçuk Mosque

But Bryer and Winfield have presented convincing evidence to show that the church was founded by Melik himself, apparently in 1223, when he gave one of his sons in marriage to the formidable Georgian Queen Rusudani (r. 1223-45). This was not the only church erected by Melik, who also built one in Bayburt and in addition contributed to the foundation of several Trapezuntine monasteries, the latter benefactions being part of the accommodation that he reached with the Grand Comnenus Andronicus I after the failure of his attempt to wrest Trebizond from Andronicus in 1223.

Here one might reflect upon the remarkable life of Melik, fifth of the eleventh sons of the Selçuk Sultan Kılıçarslan II, who at various stages in his up-and-down career found himself the vassal and virtual prisoner of two Christian sovereigns: the Armenian King Leon the Magnificent of Sissouan (r. 1187-1219) and Andronicus I Gidon of Trebizond (r. 1222-35). Melik was confined briefly by Andronicus after his failure to take Trebizond in 1223, and shortly after he was released later that year he fell into the clutches of Queen

Rusudani, to whom he owed obeisance up to the time of his death in 1225. Despite these humiliations, Melik is described in inscriptions on his buildings as "...The master of kings and sultans, Melik of Rum [Rome] and Armenia...who fights for Allah and stays on the borders making war against the enemy...." As for his foundation of churches and monasteries and the marriage of his son to the Georgian queen, a Christian, Bryer and Winfield have this to say:

> ...the churches of Bayburt and Ispir are probably the most expressive surviving monuments of the first period of this symbiosis of cultures, when a Seljuk Melik [a royal title] who set out as a Gazi and ended up as a captive and some sort of vassal first of an Armenian and then of a Greek, as a benefactor of Armenian monasteries and as an ancestor of subsequent kings of Georgia, and, as we suggest, as patron of the castle churches at Bayburt and Ispir.

Hamilton explored the castle of İspir, where, as the following passage shows, he was particularly impressed by the church and mosque that Melik had founded there:

> The castle, which I afterwards visited, is built on the right bank of the river, on a mass of porphyritic trachyte, which appears to have been rent asunder from the mass of igneous rocks forming the gorge through which the river flows. The outer walls of the castle are in ruins; these have been built of rough stones, irregularly placed together, and cased with blocks of travertine. On the summit of the rock, amidst an indiscriminate mass of ruined walls and towers, are two buildings which derive more particular notice. They are built of large hewn rocks of travertine, with joints fitting together like an Hellenic work, but although the masonry is the same they differ greatly in their style of architecture. The building near the centre of the ruins appears to have been a Greek church, having a semicircular bema at the east end, and a niche of somewhat similar appearance on each side. Its length is about sixty feet by forty in width, having a low round entrance on each side, but with no peculiar ornamental architecture about it. The

other building is smaller and square, and, from the minaret still attached to it, seems to have been a mosque. The arched entrance is enriched with arabesques, in the Saracenic style, which also prevails within; the roof is extremely elegant, resembling in a great measure the style of the most richly decorated buildings of Anni [the medieval Armenian capital]. About twelve or fourteen feet from the ground, arches spring on three sides from pilasters which fill up the corners of the room, projecting about three feet. A similar square is thus formed above the crowns of the arches, with highly enriched cornices. This square is then converted into an octagon by filling up the angles, the lower parts of which, having nothing to rest upon, are finished off with the peculiar mitre-shaped Gothic ornament and drops, so frequent at Erzeroum. The whole terminates in an octagonal conical roof.

The next stage of our journey will take us westward across the mountains from İspir, first on highway 25-79 and then on its continuation, 25-28. This takes us far up the valley of the Çoruh to Bayburt, which sits at an altitude of 1,510 meters. Here we have been following exactly the route taken by Hamilton, who spent two days riding on horseback to Bayburt. In his dairy for Friday, 24 June 1836, the first day of his ride, he writes as follows:

Notwithstanding the pressing solicitude of the Waiwode, I started at half-past seven for Baibourt, distant eighteen hours, with very bad horses, along the southern or right bank of the Tchoruk Su. To the north the valley, which is interspersed with many patches of cultivation and trees along the river side, is bounded by a lofty range of bleak and rugged hills. Two miles S. W. from İspir the river was flowing rapidly between steep hills, and our direction changed to west, passing a bridge over the Tchoruk, leading to copper mines (Bakr Maden) situated in the hills to the north, beyond which was another large stream falling into the Tchoruk Su from the N. N. W. Amongst the many wild shrubs and flowers on these hills, I was much struck with a species of honeysuckle, with which they were covered. The flower was small, and without smell, but extremely ornamental.

Medieval Castle on Hilltop near Bayburt, Print from Hamilton

Between five and six miles from Ispir we passed a road leading to the Armenian monastery of Sip [Surp, or Saint] Ovanes, and the tomb of a Turkish santon [saint] called Hussein Dede, situated about three miles to the south, amongst the limestone hills, between the ravines of which I occasionally got a glimpse of a more distant range of snowy mountains...after winding to the top of a great chain of hills on our left, we obtained a magnificent view of the deep and winding gorges which, to the west, marked the course of the Tchoruk Su, although the river itself could not there be seen; but its course was visible two or three miles to the north formed by the junction of two large rivers, the Tchoruk flowing from the west and another from the N. W.

After spending the night at the village of Karaağaç, Hamilton resumed his journey to Bayburt. When he arrived there in the afternoon he found the town still bore the scars of having been sacked by the Cossacks seven years before, during the Russian invasion of eastern Anatolia in 1828-29. Hamilton describes Bayburt as follows:

A shower of rain which fell last night had greatly refreshed the air, and we started soon after six, over undulating hills in a W. S. W. direction, slightly diverging from the Tchoruk, until we descended into a deep ravine, through which a stream flowed north... As we advanced the scenery improved greatly; our general direction was still west, over hills well covered with wood which occasionally deserved the name of timber, and about eleven A. M. we were riding through beautiful park-like scenery....At twenty minutes before four the valley again widened; the castle of Baibourt, which had been for some time visible, appeared upon an insulated rock on the other side of the river which washed its rugged base, while the hills on our left were covered with villas and gardens and bore a cheerful aspect. We crossed the Tchoruk Su by a wooden bridge below the castle, ascended the low hills which stretch to the north, and on reaching the summit found ourselves at the entrance of the ruined town. The place had been entirely destroyed, and presented a melancholy spectacle of the recklessness of Russian warfare. After traversing several ruined and deserted streets, we finally found the southern extremity of the castle hill, where the river, after flowing through part of the town, enters the rocky gorge, and having again crossed by a wooden bridge which brought us to the Armenian quarter, I soon found myself comfortably housed....

Bayburt, which was called Paipertes by the Greeks, is situated on the headwaters of the Çoruh. The town is dominated by its great acropolis rock, which is surmounted by one of the most impressive and well-preserved medieval fortresses in Anatolia. The acropolis was originally fortified by the rulers of the medieval Armenian kingdom of the Bagratid, but an ornate inscription in Arabic script records that the present fortress was completed in 1213 by Melik Mugisettin Tuğrul Şah. The original fortifications erected by Melik enclosed the town as well as the acropolis; but when the Russians attacked Bayburt in 1829 their artillery completely destroyed the lower walls of the fortress, as well as much of the town around them. The ruined church inside the citadel was done at Melik's behest around 1223, at about the same time as the church he built on the

Bayburt

acropolis of İspir. Although Bayburt was continually in Turkish hands from ca. 1072 onwards, in the Ottoman census of 1530 its population was described as 77 percent Christian, with Armenians comprising the majority of this Christian population. Up until 1624 it was the seat of a Greek Orthodox bishop, the last-surviving prelate of the Trapezuntine church south of the Pontic Alps. Hamilton decided that the church in the citadel was Greek rather than Armenian, as he notes in the following description of the fortress of Bayburt:

> Before starting for Gümüşchkhana I visited the castle of Baibourt, the ruins of which cover a considerable extent of ground, commanding the narrow pass through which the Tchoruk flows. The principal gateway faces the S.W., a considerable space being left between the inner and the outer wall, which extends lower down the hillside there than elsewhere. Over the gateway were several Turkish and Arabic inscriptions, and a large lion very rudely sculptured on each side under the arch. Near the southern extremity were the remains of a vaulted apartment, the arches of which were slightly pointed; but I was much struck with the beautiful regularity and neatness of the principal or inner wall, which was cased with square Saracenic blocks. The numerous towers along the inner wall were either square, circular, or triangular, and equally well built. Near the summit of the hill were the remains of a church which my Armenian guide confessed was Greek, of very rude construction, different from the other parts of the building, and having a semicircular bema at the east end, the wooden roof of which appeared comparatively recent. Numerous Turkish and Arabic inscriptions were carved upon the outside of the wall....This N. W. angle of the fortress is most elaborately worked and finished, the angles of the wall sloping inwards near the top. The wall is finished with a neat cornice, immediately below which is an inscription in large Arabic characters, while about fourteen feet above the ground a neat scroll runs along in a wavy line, which gives a finished and elegant appearance to the whole.

Aside from Melik's foundations, there are several other monuments in Bayburt, most notably the Ulu Cami, or Great Mosque, built by a Saltukid emir in the early thirteenth century; the Yakutiye Camii, founded by an Ilkhanid Mongol governor in 1315; and two of the conical-capped Selçuk tombs known as *kümbet*.

The next stage of our itinerary takes us from Bayburt to Gümüşhane on highway E97, a drive of 76 kilometers. Here again we are following exactly the same route as Hamilton, who in his account describes the ravages wrought upon the towns and villages of the region by the Russians during the war of 1828-29. In his diary for Saturday, 25 June 1836, he writes as follows:

> I left Baibourt at one P. M. for Gümischkhana, and reached the sum-mit of a low range of hills, extending from north to south, whence we descended into a narrow plain, opening to the north into a large tract of level country watered by the river of Balahore flowing eastward into the Tchoruk. Several villages were scattered about this plain, amongst which one was pointed out called Char, where, during the late war, 100 Russians, who had quietly entered the place after the capture of Erzeroum, were fallen upon, and massacred by the Turks. In order to avenge this unprovoked attack, General Paskewitch immediately came from Erzeroum, drove away the inhabitants, and pillaged the surrounding country. The Russians visited Baibourt three times while they had possession of Erzeroum. On the first occasion they destroyed the fortress and the houses in it; but it was not until their third visit that they destroyed the town itself, in which a Pacha had shut himself up with several thousand men....

Some eleven kilometers from Bayburt we see on our right the site of Varzahan. Today this site contains only the ruins of a medieval Armenian church that Hamilton seems to have missed when he passed this way. The church was destroyed in the nineteenth century, and its ruins are fast vanishing.

About halfway between Bayburt and Gümüşhane the highway goes over the spectacular Vaudağı pass, at an altitude of 1,878 meters. Hamilton describes the mountain scenery here in his account of the journey he made between Gümüşhane and Bayburt in May 1836:

Here began a picturesque and narrow passage between lofty limestone rocks on either side, amongst which, in searching for fossils, I could only find the fragment of a large ammonite. From hence we emerged into a plain, surrounded by high hills, still having the river, now much reduced in size, on our left, and between the thirteenth and fourteenth miles we entered another wild ravine, no less interesting for its scenery than for some of its geological details. On the left beetling cliffs rose to a stupendous height, the summit of which was fantastically broken into pinnacles and pointed rocks, on one of which were perched the ruins of a castle. On our right the river was flowing in the bottom of a deep chasm, beyond which were the same rugged limestone rocks, but not so lofty, forming an almost perfect amphitheatre, with a wild chaotic mass of rocks in the centre. As we advanced the road led over a large mass of porphyritic trachyte or trap, which, rising up in the centre, had thrown off the limestone beds in this irregular manner, and through the shattered strata of which the river has since forced its way, making at the same time a passage through the porphyritic rock beneath. The limestone cliffs on the left are at least 1500 feet above the river, and, with the picturesque castle on the summit, form a striking feature in the surrounding scenery.

We still continued the ascent of the valley, with the river on our right hand. At the seventeenth mile we entered a succession of deep and narrow gorges, amidst greenstones, traps, and other igneous rocks, until, at the twentieth mile, we reached the barren summit of the ridge or watershed which separates the streams which fall into the Tchoruk below Baibourt from those that fall into the river of the Gümischkhana; from this ridge we descended east by south into a wide and partially-cultivated valley, bounded by limestone hills on either side, in many parts horizontal, but at times offering remarkable contortions, produced by igneous rocks, protruded in several places. Not a tree was to be seen along the whole descent. At three we reached the village of Balahore, twenty-eight miles from Gümischkhane, inhabited partly by

Armenians and partly by Turks, and from whom with difficulty we procured even a few eggs.

The castle mentioned by Hamilton has given its name to the village of Kale, which in Turkish means "castle or fortress." The village is just to the west of the above-mentioned pass, where we see the ruins of a medieval fortress rising to a height of 250 meters over the north side of the road. This is known as Keçi Kalesi, or Goat Castle, identified as the citadel of Mesochaldia, a Byzantine stronghold that was later rebuilt by the Grand Comneni of Trebizond. As its name implies (in Greek the prefix *meso* means "in the middle"), Mesochaldia was at the heart of Chaldia, which at first had been a theme of the Byzantine Empire, and then, at a later period, and in a much diminished state, of the Empire of the Grand Comneni of Trebizond. Chaldia is one of the most ancient regional names on the map of Anatolia. Arnold Toynbee says that "for an interpretation of the name Chaldia [the classical scholar] will have to go back to Urartian, Assyrian, and Achaemenian records of the eighth, seventh, and sixth centuries BC." In their book, *The People of the Hills*, C. Burney and D. M. Lang refer to the Chaldians, as "almost certainly the descendants or remnants of the Urartians."

Some five kilometers north of Kale the village of Kabaköy has been identified as the ancient Lerin. The village mosque was formerly a church dedicated to Haghia Sophia. As it has been dated to the sixth century, it is one of the oldest churches in northwestern Anatolia.

The story of the Christian community of Lerin in late Ottoman times reflects the turmoil that existed in eastern Anatolia during that period. The Tanzimat, or Reform Movement, which officially began with the signing of the Gülhane decree by Sultan Abdülmecit on 3 November 1839, promised religious freedom for all subjects of the Ottoman Empire, Christians and Jews, as well as Muslims. Many former Christians in eastern Anatolia who had converted to Islam while retaining their original religion in secret, the so-called crypto-Christians, were led by the Tanzimat reforms to come out into the open with their true religious beliefs. In 1857 half of the population of Lerin, which then numbered some 200, suddenly revealed that they had been crypto-Christians. They and many others in the Pontus, then renounced Islam and openly espoused Christianity, and during the next generation half a dozen new churches were built in the region between Lerin and Gümüşhane. These churches were all abandoned after the population exchange of 1923, when the remaining Christians of the region, probably reconverted to Islam. Today the ruins of these late nineteenth-century churches stand starkly in the surrounding landscape, the last monuments of the Christians of Chaldia.

Eight kilometers beyond Kale there is a turnoff on the left for highway 885, which leads south to Erzincan via the Kösedağı Pass, which is some 20 kilometers to the south at an altitude of 1,910 meters. This pass gave its name to the battle of Kösedağ, fought there on 26 June 1242. In this battle the Mongols decisively defeated the Selçuks and thus brought their preeminence in Anatolia to an end.

Seventeen kilometers beyond this turnoff we come to Gümüşhane, our route taking us along the upper reaches of the Harşit Çayı. The present Gümüşhane is a creation of the Turkish Republic, replacing the original town of the same name, now known as Eski (Old) Gümüşhane, abandoned after its Greek inhabitants departed in the population exchange of 1923. Eski Gümüşhane has a number of ruined monuments from both the Byzantine and early Turkish periods. These include several Byzantine churches that were converted to mosques, some of them with wall paintings, as well as an Ottoman mosque of the mid-sixteenth century, the Süleymaniye Camii, and several old *hamam*s and *han*s.

Gümüşhane means "Silver House" or "Mint," a name deriving from the silver mines that existed here in former times, and which Marco Polo remarked upon when he passed this way in 1296. Until the nineteenth century the Greeks called it Argyropolis, or Silver City. The mines of Marco Polo's time would have been near Eski Gümüşhane, where the worked-out shafts are still guarded by the impressive ruins of Tzanicha Castle, mentioned by Procopius. The castle stands on a great spur of rock two kilometers north of modern Gümüşhane, perched some 400 meters above the Harşit Çayı. Within the castle there are the remains of a Byzantine chapel with well-preserved wall paintings from the time of the Grand Comneni of Trebizond.

The silver mines of Gümüşhane were still being worked in Hamilton's time, when, though almost moribund, they were nevertheless the principal source of that metal in the Ottoman Empire, as well as of a small quantity of gold. Hamilton writes of Gümüşhane as follows:

> The silver-mines of Gümischkhana (silver-house) have the reputation of being the richest and most important mines of the type in the Turkish dominions. The town is also considered as a seminary for the instruction of miners throughout Turkey; and I have been constantly told, in very distant parts of Asia Minor, when making inquiries respecting mines in the neighbourhood, either that the miners came from Gümischkhana, or that a connexion of some kind or another existed between it and Gümischkhana; besides which the director of mines here is considered as the superintendent and chief of all the mining districts in Anatolia....
>
> The only mine now worked is situated about a mile and a half to the S. E. of Gümischkhana, beyond the hills which surround the town....It was not shafted up at all, the galleries being only supported by the natural rock. The direction of the principal shaft sloped 20 degrees to the south, but other galleries branched out in all directions, sometimes spreading into capacious chambers, at others passing through long and narrow passages, and either descending perpendicular chasms, or proceeding onwards horizontally. In one of these chambers the wet ground sloped to a vast lake or reservoir of great depth, beyond which I could distinguish by the light of their lamps several workmen removing the rock wall itself for the sake of the ore it contained. On the whole there appeared to be neither method, order, nor prudence in the manner in which they worked. The best ore is found in lumps or nodules in the middle of the vein, consisting of a soft black clay,

which also contains a small quantity of metal. The whole face of the hill near this mine was covered with the remains of old workings and galleries, in which the ore had been exhausted.

In another interesting passage Hamilton gives us his observations concerning Armenians who dwelt in caves in the region around Gümüşhane. He writes as follows:

We left Gümischkhana at five [A. M.], and, after crossing to the right bank of the river, ascended the valley E. by S. for nearly six miles; at first between a succession of beautiful gardens and orchards. When we were clear of the gardens, the air was deliciously scented with the perfume of a tree in full flower growing abundantly along the banks of the river. In appearance it closely resembled the willow; the leaves had the same colour and the same luminosity on the under side; the smell of the yellow flower, which was small and cruciform, resembled that of the jessamine, and although I occasionally found it wild in other parts of Asia Minor, it was long before I discovered it was the jijiva, or jujube tree. I should, however, think it must be sufficiently hardy to grow in England, where it would be a great ornament. The low, flat-roofed and almost subterranean houses had a strange appearance; built against the steep hill side, they require only one wall in front to support the roof, which on the other three sides rests on the ground. Like many of the Armenian villages, these hovels are so low that you may ride on the roof without knowing where you are....Near the eighth mile we halted to allow the baggage horses to come up with us at an Armenian blacksmith's forge. I have seldom seen such a wild and savage-looking set of beings. For some time we could not make out who or what they were: by degrees, however, we learnt that they were Christians, although they seemed afraid of confessing their religion....

Hamilton's description reminds us of what Xenophon, who passed through this part of Anatolia in 400 B.C. with the Ten Thousand, had to say about these cave dwellers. This part of their journey took them through a group of Armenian villages where, in contrast to the hostility they had met with in passing through Kurdistan, they were received with truly Anatolian hospitality. In his *Anabasis* Xenophon has this to say about these Armenians:

> Their houses were underground, the entrances like the mouth of a well, but spacious below; there were passages dug into them for cattle, but the people descended into them by ladders. In the houses were goats, sheep, cows, and fowls, with their young; all the cattle were kept on fodder within the walls. There was also wheat, barley, vegetables and barley-wine in large bowls...the liquor was very strong, unless one mixed water with it, and a very pleasant drink for those who were accustomed to it....The chief man...to show his goodwill, pointed out where some wine was buried. This night therefore, the soldiers [the Greeks] rested in their several quarters in the midst of great abundance.

The next stage of our itinerary will take us from Gümüşhane to Torul, a drive of 25 kilometers. As we leave Gümüşhane yellow archaeological signposts point the way to two monuments in the vicinity: Canca Kale and Olucak Monastery. Canca Kale appears to have been a fortress of the Trapezuntine Empire. Olucak Monastery was dedicated to St. John Prodromos, the Forerunner. It was founded around 1710 as a convent, but by 1914 the nuns had been replaced by monks. The present church at Olucak was built in 1859, during that period when the crypto-Christians of the area were openly proclaiming their Christianity.

The highway continues along the valley of the Harşit Çayı, which here has the grandeur of a canyon. At the confluence of the Harşit and one of its tributaries we come to Torul, where we will pause before we turn south to go over the Zigana Pass toward the coast.

Torul is the ancient Ardasa, of which the only remnant is the ruined castle above the town. Ardasa had the distinction of being the last stronghold of Byzantium. Fatih was unable to take the castle here when he besieged and captured Trebizond in 1461. The defenders at Ardasa held out until the winter of 1479-80, when they finally surrendered to an Ottoman force under Fatih's eldest son, the future Beyazit II.

The castle at Ardasa is mentioned by Clavijo, who calls it Cadaca. Clavijo and his party stopped here after going over the Zigana Pass in the spring of 1404. In what follows Clavijo describes their journey over the mountain defile, where they had stopped at a castle that he calls Zegan, the stronghold that guarded the Zigana Pass:

> The road was excellent, except in one part where from the height above a landslide had taken place, damming back a stream. This place we only managed to pass after much touble and delay: whereby that day's march proved short, for the cause aforesaid. That night we had to camp out in the open. Tuesday [29 April 1404], next day, the stream led over very high mountains, where there was snow and we had many streams to cross. By nightfall we had come up with a castle called Zegan, built on a high peak. The sole entrance thereto was by a wooden bridge that was stretched from a neighbouring rock to the castle gate. This stronghold was garrisoned by the men of a Greek noble whose name was Cyril Cabasica....

Cyril Cabasica was actually Kyr (Lord) Leon Kabazites, Duke of the Trapezuntine theme of Chaldia. Kabazites was not in the castle at the Zigana Pass at the time, but Clavijo and his party would meet the Duke at Ardasa two days later. Clavijo continues:

> ...we came to a castle that stood crowning a height that lay across and blocking our road, the name of which was Cadace [Ardasa]. At the foot of the castle and the height flowed a river, while on the other shore stood a range of bare mountains that none would attempt to make his way over. Thus the road was but a narrow strait passing between the river on one side and the rock of the castle on the other, and the passage was exceedingly close, one man, or one horse at a time only being able to make way ahead. Hence though only a few might be on guard in the castle, they could easily stop any number going that road: which to cross this mountain range was the only path

by which the march could be made. From this stronghold therefore there now came forth a band of men who demanded toll of our party and were intent to levy customs on the baggage that we were carrying along with us and this we had to pay. The place indeed belongs to the lord Cabasica...and there he had quartered his band of brigands and evil folk, for that lord is a man of evil sort....

Clavijo and his party finally met the duke the next day, after they had stopped at yet another of his castles, whose ruins can still be seen 14 kilometers southeast of Torul. This was the castle of Golacha, the ducal capital of Chaldia, where Kyr Leon Kabazites was waiting for them, as they soon learned.

...we received notice that the lord of these lands...was at this very time in residence here: we therefore sent our dragoman [interpreter] to give him information as to who we were, although in fact this lord already knew all that was needful concerning us, news having been sent forward to him as to ourselves and our embassy from the other castles in the

Way Station for Hungry Travelers, Zigana Pass

territory by which we had already passed. No sooner, therefore, had we sent in our messenger than a man came forward from the castle on horseback, with a message from the lord enjoining us immediately to halt....

The messenger informed them that they would be allowed to camp near the castle for the night if they both paid the duke a toll and presented him with a present. Clavijo writes of his meeting the duke as follows:

...the next day, Thursday [1 May 1400], in the forenoon the lord [Kabazites] issued from his stronghold, appearing at our camping place, and accompanying him were thirty of his horsemen, armed with bows and arrows. He was mounted on a fine horse, and he too held in his hands arrows with his bow....He then proceeded to explain to us that he had lived in that barren land, where we now found him at peace, but that he had continually to defend himself against the Turks who were his neighbours on all sides, against whom he was ever at war. Further he said he and his men had nothing to live on, except it were what they could get given to them by those who passed through their country, or what they could come by plundering the lands of their neighbours, and hence he must now implore us to give him some aid as a free gift in the form of money or goods.

Clavijo satisfied Kabazites with a gold cup and some of their supplies, after which he and his party were allowed to pass, although they were halted at yet another of the Duke's castles the following day. But after that they were stopped no more, having passed through this no-man's-land of Chaldia, where the march warriors of the Emperor of Trebizond had been fighting the Turks for nearly two centuries. A descendant of Leon Kabazites was in command of the castle of Ardasa when it finally surrendered to Prince Selim in the winter of 1479-80, when the long history of Byzantium finally came to an end in this remote fortress above the Zigana Pass.

After leaving Torul there is a choice of two parallel routes for the first half of the way down to Trabzon, either the new superhighway E97, which goes through a tunnel at the highest point of the mountain, or the old highway 885, which goes over the Zigana Pass. We will take the latter route, which goes over the pass at an altitude of 2,010 meters, the famous Pontic Gates that have been the terror of travelers since time immemorial, with whole caravans sometimes frozen to death when they were caught there by blizzards.

After going over the pass the road takes us steadily down the valley of the river known in antiquity as the Prytanis, now an upper branch of the Değirmendere, which joins its lower branch, the ancient Pyxitis, at Maçka. We have on an earlier itinerary already travelled along this last stretch of the route, from Maçka to Trabzon, and so now we can just relax and look ahead for the first sight of the Black Sea. This was the route taken by the Ten Thousand on the final leg of their long trek across eastern Anatolia, as they looked ahead for their first glimpse of the Euxine, the Hospitable Sea. Xenophon describes this emotional scene in Book II of his *Anabasis:*

On the fifth day they reached the mountain, the name of which was Theces. No sooner had the men in front ascended it and caught sight of the sea than a great cry arose, and Xenophon, with the rear guard, catching the sound of it, conjectured that another set of enemies must surely be attacking in front; for they were followed by the inhabitants of the country, which was all aflame; indeed the rear guard had killed some and captured others alive by laying an ambuscade; they had also taken about twenty wicker shields, covered with the raw hides of shaggy oxen.

But as the shout became louder and nearer, and those who from time to time came up, began racing at the top of their speed towards the shouters, and the shouting continually recommenced with yet greater volume as the numbers increased, Xenophon settled in his mind that something extraordinary must have happened, so he mounted his horse, taking with him Lycius and the cavalry, and he galloped to the rescue. Presently they could hear the soldiers shouting and passing on the joyful word, "The sea! the sea!"

Xenophon

Thereupon they began running, the rearguard and all, and the baggage animals and horses came galloping up. But when they had reached the summit, then indeed they fell to embracing one another - generals and officers and all - and the tears trickled down their cheeks. And on a sudden, some one, whoever it was, having passed down the order, the soldiers began bringing stones and erecting a great cairn, whereupon they dedicated a host of untanned skins, and staves, and captured wicker shields, and with his own hand the guide hacked the shields to pieces, inviting the rest to follow his example. After this the Hellenes dismissed the guide with a present raised from the common store, to wit, a horse, a silver bowl, a Persian dress, and ten darics [Persian coins]; but what he most begged to have were their rings, and of these he got several from the soldiers. So, after pointing out to them a village where they could find quarters, and the road by which they should proceed towards the land of the Macrones, as evening fell he turned his back upon them and was gone.

And thus the last of our itineraries in the Black Sea region comes to and end, with the blue waters of the sea and the towers of Trebizond spread out before us.

SELECT BIBLIOGRAPHY

Ainsworth, William F. *Travels and Researches in Asia Minor, Mesopotamia, Chaldea and Armenia.* London, 1842.

Apollonius Rhodius. *Argonautica (The Voyage of Argo).* Translated by E. V. Rieu. Harmondsworth, England, 1959.

Bryer, Anthony, and Winfield, David. *The Byzantine Monuments and Topography of the Pontus.* 2 vols. Washington, D.C. 1985.

Burney, C. and Lang, R. M. *The People of the Hills.* London, 1974.

Clavijo, Ruy Gonzalez de. *Embassy to Tamerlane.* Translated by Guy le Strange. London, 1926.

Evliya Çelebi. *Seyahatname (Narrative of Travels).* Translated by Joseph von Hammer. London, 1834.

Constantine VII. *Porphyrogenitus, The Imperial Administration.* Translated by R. J. H. Jenkins. Washington, D.C., 1967.

Diogenes Laertius. *Lives of the Eminent Philosophers.* 2 vols. Translated by R. D. Hicks. London, 1925.

Djobadze, Wachtang. *Early Medieval Georgian Monasteries in Historic Tao, Klarjeti, and Şavşeti.* Stuttgart, 1992.

Gyllius, Petrus. *The Thracian Bosphorus* (in Latin). Lyon, 1561.

Hamilton, William J. *Researches in Asia Minor, Pontus and Armenia.* London, 1842.

Herodotus, *The History.* Translated by Aubrey de Selincourt. Harmondsworth, England, 1954.

Homer, *The Iliad.* Translated by Richmond Lattimore. Chicago, 1951.

Lang, David Marshall. *The Georgians.* New York, 1966.

Macaulay, Rose. *The Towers of Trebizond.* London, 1956.

Millet, Gabriel and Rice, David Talbot. *Byzantine Painting at Trebizond.* London, 1936.

Nişanyan, Sevan. *Zoom In-Black Sea.* Istanbul, 1990.

Procopius of Caesarea. *The Wars and the Edifices.* 7 vols. Translated by H. B. Dewing and Glanville Downey. London, 1954.

Schiltberger, Johannes. *Bondage and Travels in Europe, Asia and Africa 1396-1427.* Translated by J. Buchan Telfer. London, 1879

Stoneman, Richard. *Across the Hellespont.* London, 1987.

Strabo. *Geography.* Vol. 5. Translated by H. L. Jones. Cambridge, Massachusetts, 1928.

Talbot Rice, David. *The Church of Haghia Sophia at Trebizond.* Edinburgh, 1968.

Xenophon. *The Anabasis.* Translated by Carleton C. Brownson. London, 1922.

INDEX

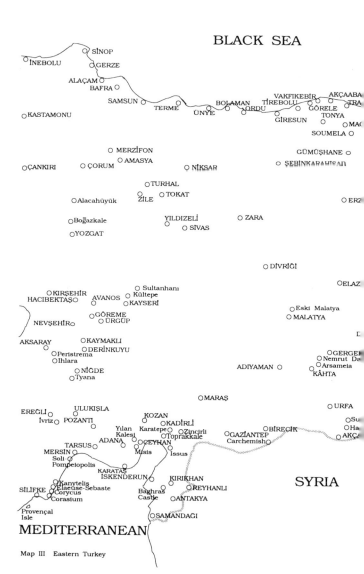

BLACK SEA

SİNOP
GERZE
İNEBOLU
ALAÇAM
BAFRA
KASTAMONU
SAMSUN
TERME
ÜNYE
BOLAMAN
ORDU
VAKFIKEBİR
TİREBOLU
GÖRELE
TONYA
GİRESUN
AKÇAABA
TRA
MA(
SOUMELA

MERZİFON
AMASYA
NİKSAR
GÜMÜŞHANE
ŞEBİNKARAHİSAR
ÇANKIRI
ÇORUM

TURHAL
TOKAT
ZİLE
Alacahüyük

ERZ

Boğazkale
YILDIZELİ
SİVAS
ZARA
YOZGAT

DİVRİĞİ

ELAZ

KIRŞEHİR
HACIBEKTAŞ
AVANOS
Sultanhanı
Kültepe
KAYSERİ
GÖREME
ÜRGÜP
NEVŞEHİR

Eski Malatya
MALATYA

AKSARAY
KAYMAKLI
DERİNKUYU
Peristrema
Ihlara
NİĞDE
Tyana
ADIYAMAN

GERGE
Nemrut Da
Arsameia
KÂHTA

MARAŞ
URFA
EREĞLİ
ULUKIŞLA
İvriz
POZANTI
KOZAN
KADİRLİ
Yılan
Karatepe
Zincirli
Kalesi
Toprakkale
ADANA
CEYHAN
Misis
Issus
TARSUS
MERSİN
Soli
Pompeiopolis
KARATAŞ
İSKENDERUN
KIRIKHAN
REYHANLI
Baghras
Castle
ANTAKYA
GAZİANTEP
Carchemish
BİRECİK
Su
Ha
AKÇ

Kanytelis
Elaeuse-Sebaste
Corycus
Corasium
SİLİFKE
SYRIA

Provençal
Isle
SAMANDAĞI

MEDITERRANEAN

Map III Eastern Turkey